four empire

● ● ● ellipsis

four empires of islam

imperial achievement

First published 1998 by
●●●ellipsis
2 Rufus Street
London
N1 6PE
EMAIL ...@ellipsis.co.uk

ISBN 1 899858 44 X

Publisher Tom Neville
Designed by Jonathan Moberly
Edited by Vicky Wilson
Photographs by Christopher Tadgell, except page 88 by
Virginia Fass, page 197 by Charles Neale
Layout and image processing by Heike Löwenstein
Drawings by John Hewitt
Glossary by Andrew Wyllie
Index by Diana LeCore
Printed and bound in Hong Kong

British Library Cataloguing in Publication Data: a catalogue
record for this publication is available from the British Library

contents

By the middle of the 13th century Mongol hordes – led by the devastating Genghis Khan (1206–27) and his successors – had swept through Asia and eastern Europe. But the nomadic Mongols were no more able to rule a vast, rapidly amassed empire than the Arabs before them, and equally rapidly they succumbed to it. A power vacuum was left in central Asia and Iran – where the unorthodox Shi'ite branch of Islam (which maintained that the line of legitimate succession as imam or leader lay with the descent of the Prophet Muhammad's blood through his daughter Fatima and her husband Ali rather than through election, as did the orthodox Sunnis) remained the strongest faction. The vacuum was filled by Timur, surnamed i-Leng ('the Lame', hence Tamburlaine).[1]

This extraordinary figure was born in 1336 of a supposed descendant of Genghis Khan and a Turkish mother at Kish (modern Shahr-i Sabz) near Samarkand in the region then known as Transoxiana. Many adventures and much duplicity led Timur to power at Samarkand in 1370. Proclaiming himself the restorer of the Mongol empire, he championed the khans of the

1 **Timur in his tent palace** (16th-century miniature).

Golden Horde – which under Genghis Khan's grand-son Batu had taken Russia in the 1230s – and occupied Moscow in 1380. Constantly campaigning, he then turned on Iran, where chaos had followed the death of Abu Said, the last Ilkhanid successor of Genghis Khan's grandson Hulagu, in 1335. Khurasan and the other eastern provinces were his within two years, most of the rest by 1387. Pushing on through Mesopotamia, he was the dominant power in the Caucasus by 1395.

Much of what had survived the Mongols – preserved by their more civilised Ilkhanid descendants – was destroyed by Timur. Rebellions in Persia attracted particularly savage vengeance. So too did the Tughluq sultans of Delhi, and Timur cut a swathe into India to destroy both city and sultanate in 1398. The Mamluks of Egypt and the Ottomans of Turkey were the next prey: the former were defeated at Damascus in 1400, the latter in Anatolia in 1402. Egypt and Byzantium offered submission and Timur turned towards China, but died on the way in 1405.

Timur assigned Herat and eastern Persia to his son Shahrukh, Tabriz and the west to his son Miranshah, and Fars and the south to his grandson Pir Muhammad. Miranshah died in 1407 and Shahrukh managed to unite east and west after a protracted struggle. He fostered prosperity and took Herat to new brilliance before he died in 1447. His learned son Ulugh Beg, who had been the equally enlightened governor of Transoxiana, sustained his legacy for only two years before his assassination. The Uzbek Turks took Transoxiana and rival confederacies of Turkoman tribes, known as the Black and White Sheep, fought for the rest. The White Sheep ultimately emerged predominant but excited the opposition of the Ottomans and lost the empire to chaos in the west. The Timurids regained Khurasan, and Herat's brilliance was revived under Husein Baykara (1469–1504).

In devastated Persia, meanwhile, underground resistance was fomented by fraternities of holy men (sufis) formed for the veneration of particular saints. The most radical, naturally, were Shi'ite. Of these, the Safavids – founded by one Safi ud-Din, who claimed descent from Ali through the imams – enrolled bands of Turkomans as soldiers in their cause. Caught up in the conflict between the Black and White Sheep, the Safavids expanded their following and were led to their first great victory by Safi's descendant Ismail, who took Tabriz from the White Sheep in 1502.

Ismail proclaimed himself Shah and, promoting Shi'ism, proceeded to absorb the western provinces of the former Timurid empire, left in chaos by the White Sheep. On the death of Husein Baykara, the Sunni Uzbeks of Transoxiana invaded Khurasan. Ismail challenged them there and won the province. A vigorous Shi'ite in possession of the heartlands of the former Seljuk empire, he now excited the opposition of the staunchly Sunni Ottomans and lost his capital, Tabriz, to the overwhelming forces of Selim I. Selim was forced to withdraw by mutinous troops but annexed northern Mesopotamia. Ismail never recovered from the blow and died in 1524, but reverse only stiffened Shi'ite resolve.

Iran reasserted its cultural pre-eminence in central and southern Asia during the long reign of Ismail's son Tahmasp (1524–76).[2] However, recurrent conflict with the Ottomans sapped Safavid strength. An uneasy truce had been reached by the time of Tahmasp's death, but then dynastic rivalry reduced Iran to chaos. From it – and relative obscurity – miraculously emerged Shah Abbas I, who took the Safavids to their

2 **Isfahan, fresco of Shah Tahmasp receiving the exiled Moghul emperor of India, Humayun, in a chihil sutun ('many-columned' pavilion)**.

apogee in another long reign (1587–1629). After a series of reverses inflicted by both Ottomans and Uzbeks, the shah availed himself of the expertise of envoys from Elizabethan England to replace inefficient and unruly tribal levies with a professional army. Pitting it against the Ottomans for the first time in 1603, he ejected them from Tabriz and went on to regain most of the territory lost since the initial defeat of Shah Ismail.

A great administrator and magnificent builder, Abbas I founded a new capital beside old Seljuk Isfahan and endowed it with several of the world's most superb mosques. There was disaster under his malevolent successor, but recovery and more splendid building under Abbas II (1642–66). The glory reflected on his successor, Shah Suleiman, but hid stagnation. Renewed conflict with the Ottomans and clashes with India over Kandahar and Russia over the Caucasus undermined the later Safavids, especially Shah Sultan Husein (1696–1722), who was forced to abdicate by Afghan usurpers. A nationalist revival led to chaos until a Khurasanian adventurer seized the throne as Nadir Shah in 1736 and promoted the spectacular revival of Persian fortune.

Palaces

Little of substance survives of Timurid or early Safavid palaces. The Akserai palace at Timur's birthplace, Kish, seems to have followed the four-iwan court tradition descending from the Parthians (see volume 4, IMPERIAL SPACE, page 98). One of the iwans survives in part: it is the earliest known example flanked by minaret-like towers rising from the ground instead of perched on an applied frontispiece (pishtaq). By contrast, the Bagh-i-Maydan palace at Samarkand seems to have consisted of a succession of walled gardens (chahar baghs) with canals and pavilions – an image of earthly paradise in which an enclosed square is divided into quarters by four rivers flowing in the cardinal directions from the source of the waters of life in the centre. The Spanish ambassador to Timur's court, Gonzales de Clavijo, related the Bagh-i-Maydan to the tent palaces which housed the monarch on his campaigns (see 1, page 6) and which, of course, descend from the tent palaces of the Achaemenids (see volume 1, ORIGINS, page 218).

The first Mughal emperor Babur describes the most celebrated element of the Bagh-i-Maydan, the chihil sutun ('many-columned' pavilion), as square

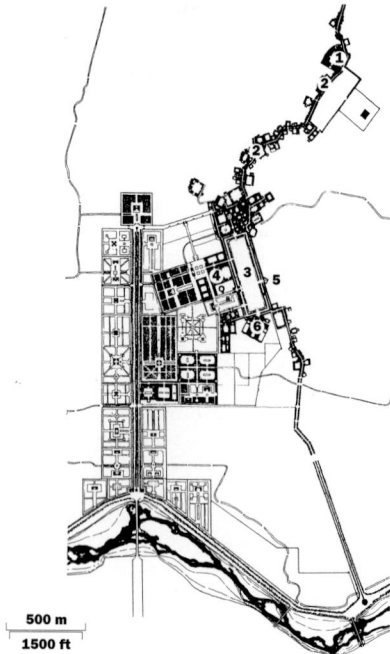

500 m
1500 ft

3 **Safavid Isfahan** plan.

(1) Seljuk Friday mosque; (2) souks; (3) Safavid maidan; (4) palace; (5) Lutfullah (palatine) mosque; (6) Masjid-i Shah (congregational mosque).

To the east of the garden was a vast oblong parade and polo ground (maidan) – 521 by 160 metres (1709 by 525 feet) – oriented with its short sides to the north and south. Shah Abbas I rebuilt the palace, extended the gardens and enlarged the maidan, surrounding it with shopping arcades linking the congregational mosque to the south, the palatine mosque to the east and the main souk to the north where junction was effected with the Seljuk town. To the west of the palace garden, at an acute angle to it and the main axis of the maidan, the main artery of the new town ran due south to the river, where it continued over the first of several magnificent covered bridges.

with corner towers and four two-storey portals
which led to a cruciform central hall. This was a
latter-day apadana derived from the ancient
Achaemenid tradition (see volume 3, IMPERIAL FORM,
page 12). Babur also describes the Tareb Khana in
the palace at Herat as having four subsidiary chambers on the diagonals in addition to vestibules on the
main axes. This represents the garden-palace building type known as hasht behisht ('eight paradises', no
doubt because of the eight splendidly embellished
chambers opening from the central octagon). A hasht
behisht was added c. 1468 to the Tabriz palace of
Uzun Hassan. The type will play an important part in
our history.

The forms described by the visitors to Timur's
court clearly subsist in the later Safavid palace of the
new Isfahan inaugurated by Shah Abbas I in 1598.
The plan of the town[3] takes advantage of an
open site already developed by Shah Ismail with a palace
and gardens in the rectangular tradition of the
earthly paradise. The principal elements of the
palace[4] are the main gate and place of appearance

4 **Isfahan, palace** (early 18th-century engraving).

5 Isfahan, palace, Ali Kapu.
The columned portico is raised over a high basement in which access to the palace from the maidan crosses the shopping arcade. Over two basement storeys are three more for the principal apartments, but much of the space is given to a grand double-height hall rising from the same level and to the same height as the portico.

6 **Isfahan, palace, Ali Kapu** music-room vault.
The joinery of the columned portico was gilded.
The intricate interior of the top-floor music room,
deeply recessed with vase-shaped niches, was stuccoed
and painted to resemble an extremely refined garden
alive with birds.

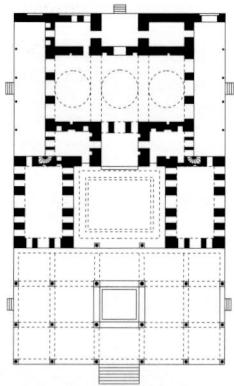

7 **Isfahan, palace, Chihil Sutun** plan.

The audience hall with porticos to north and south, iwans east and west, seems to have been built by Shah Abbas I before the end of the 16th century. The central chambers framing an enlarged throne iwan and the portico of 20 columns before it to the east were added under Abbas II (1642–66). Fountains in the throne iwan and the columned portico fed a canal which ran on into the main pool – and just as water linked inside with out, so it doubled the portico by reflection ('chihil' may mean 40 or many).

known as Ali Kapu[5-6] on the west side of the open
parade ground (maidan), and the main audience hall
known as Chihil Sutun.[7-8] Both are columned porticos (talars) derived from the apadana. Both provided
residential accommodation on several storeys behind
the columns, but Shah Abbas I reputedly preferred to
live mainly in the Ali Kapu. To the many other buildings which once enclosed courts and enjoyed gardens, Shah Suleiman added a hasht behisht.[9-10] Most
Iranian cities benefited from Safavid patronage – as
did the imperial arteries and the merchants of the
age.[11-12]

8 OVERLEAF **Isfahan, palace, Chihil Sutun.**
   The woodwork was gilded, with walls and vaults
plastered and painted with stylised floral motifs, as usual.
The exterior has aberrant murals in a pseudo-western style;
the main interior walls of the great hall follow Timurid
precedent (recorded by Babur), with murals representing
episodes from the dynasty's history in an inflated indigenous
style (see 2, page 11). Tile played a now depleted part, but
mirror mosaic remains the dominant element in the east-
facing throne iwan behind the great columned portico.

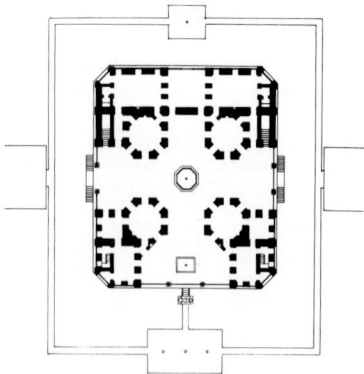

9 Isfahan, palace, hasht behisht of Shah Suleiman (1666–94), plan.

Inserted at the centre of Shah Abbas' Nightingale Garden, Shah Suleiman's garden pavilion presumably recalled its greater predecessors at Herat and Tabriz. The 'eight paradises' were the gorgeously decorated rooms on two levels in each of the four diagonal wings, flanking columned porticos to south, west and east and an iwan to the north.

10 **Isfahan, palace, hasht behisht of Shah Suleiman**
central octagon vault.

The muqarnas – a honeycomb-like web formed from
squinches multiplied to a reduced scale – retain some
original florid plasterwork and mirror mosaic. Water
channelled from the fountain in the centre of the octagon
highlighted the unconstrained devolution of space from
inside to out.

11 Caravanserai at Dihbid on the Yazd–Kerman road.
The vast majority of Safavid caravanserai (hostels for traders) conformed to the traditional square plan – like the one associated with the Madrasa-yi Madar-i Shah (now a hotel) in Isfahan – but there was some experimentation.

12 Bukhara, merchant house.

In many of the most opulent merchant houses in Transoxiana, as in Iran, the court was addressed by a palatial columned portico instead of an iwan.

Tombs and shrines

The most important Timurid tomb, the Gir-i Amir of
Timur himself at Samarkand,[13-14] consists of iwan
and domed chamber (qubba), octagonal outside,
square inside with the arms of a Greek cross projecting through iwans from the square – a domed version
of the courtyard of the funerary complex of Sultan
Hasan in Cairo (see volume 6, FOUR CALIPHATES, pages
164–65). A high drum with an exaggerated inner cav-
ity raises the semi-bulbous outer dome way above the
inner one. Exaggeratedly high drums and/or frontispieces were to be as characteristic of Timurid tombs
as bulbous, cannelled domes: in Samarkand several
works in the Shah-i Zinda necropolis compensate for
the prime example, the largely lost Ishrat Khaneh.[15-16]

Instead of the square and cross of the main space –
as in the Gir-i Amir or the Ishrat Khaneh – later
Timurid and early Safavid planners of works such as
the tomb of Mullah Hassan at Sultaniya[17] revised the
octagonal form of the tomb of the Ilkhanid ruler
Oljeitu (1304–16, see volume 6, FOUR CALIPHATES,
page 145), added subsidiary chambers to each side and
projected the great internal arcade on to the exterior.
The tomb became a hasht behisht – or rather the hasht

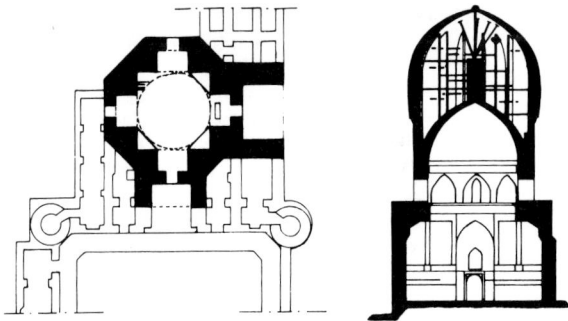

13 **Samarkand, Gir-i Amir** 1404, plan and section.

14 **Samarkand, Gir-i Amir.**

Originally ordered for one of Timur's grandsons, Muhammad Sultan (d. 1402), the tomb chamber was built in association with the monastery (khanaqah) of a sufi saint. Finished towards the end of 1404 (after rebuilding to a greater height than originally planned), it received Timur himself less than three months later and then became the dynasty's mausoleum. The addition of a madrasa (college) to the north in 1434 altered the original front, but the minarets were detached from the iwan frontispiece and placed at the ends of screen walls. Much of the original brickwork survives on the other three unencumbered sides. Tiles – or rather glazed bricks – are used sparingly to form an irregular diagonal grid on the main walls. The drum has a huge Cufic inscription in multi-coloured tiles and the ribbed dome is blue. Inside, a dado of hexagonal tiles in alabaster is surmounted by a band of script in jasper. The suspended vault is painted ostentatiously in blue and gold.

Slightly earlier (1394), a rather more complex plan was devised for the sufi Sheikh Ahad Yasavi in Turkestan: possibly doubling as a madrasa and tomb, there are chambers (including the tomb) beyond the iwan in each of the four sides of the central domed cube and a variety of halls (including a mosque) in the corners.

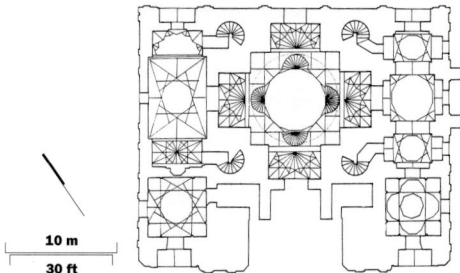

15 **Samarkand, Ishrat Khaneh** c. 1460, plan and section.

Attributed to Habibah Sultan, principal wife of the late Timurid ruler Abu Said, the complex plan suggests the tomb was designed for numerous members of her family: the rectangular hall to the west may have been for obsequies, the central and subsidiary domed chambers would doubtless have contained cenotaphs, the actual burial sarcophagi would have been the crypt. A further elaboration of the plan, providing oblong halls to all four sides of a square central space and square rooms in the corners, was devised for Abu Said's son Ulugh Beg Miranshah, king of Kabul 1469–94. Most of the façade is screened by the frontispiece. The saucer dome (and tall blind drum of the outer dome)

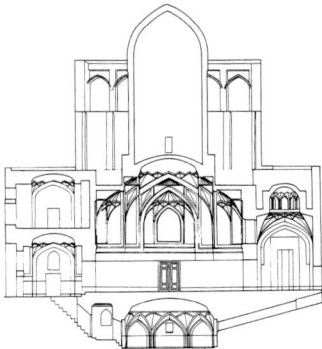

are carried on a lattice vault generated from the
combination of square and Greek cross: the arches framing
the outside and inside of each arm are echoed, amplifed,
across the main space between the imposts of their
neighbours; to support the central dome, a network of
fragmentary arches connects the main ones to form a
staccato series of triangular and lozenge-shaped squinches
which echo the lower ones in the corners between the arms.
The idea seems to have been tested c. 1417 in the tomb
chamber of the Gauhar Shad madrasa at Herat.

16 Samarkand, Shah-i Zinda necropolis.
Many of the Shah-i Zinda tombs are decorated with
blue-, white- and yellow-glazed tiles moulded to produce
patterns in low relief. Inside, also sumptuously tiled, the
main chambers are usually covered with semi-circular or
octagonal domes.

17 **Sultaniya, tomb of Mullah Hassan** 1530.

Earlier approximations to the hasht behisht form include
the tomb of Khwaja Abu Nasir at Balkh (c. 1460), where
the cross-in-square survives in plan but is converted to
an octagon by squinches supporting the dome, and the
chamfered sides of the exterior mass have deep niches on
two levels between the four axial iwans.

18 **Qumm, shrine of Fatima** (the eighth imam Reza's sister, who died in 816).

Often sited in or beside the compound of a mosque or at least incorporating a prayer hall, the principal mausoleum (with its ambulatory for pilgrims) is the nucleus of an extensive complex which includes subsidiary tomb chambers for those fortunate enough to be buried in the orbit of grace emitted by the imam or his relative, a Koranic recitation room and facilities for propagating Shi'ite dogma.

19 **Samarra, shrine of imams Ali al-Hadi and his son Hassan al-Askari.**

20 **Isfahan, shrine of Harun-i Vilayet** early Safavid, screened sepulchre.

behisht became a tomb – ideally set in the paradise of a chahar bagh. In fact there were no grand imperial Safavid mausoleums in Iran. Much money and attention was, however, lavished on the shrines of imams and Shi'ite saints (imamzada) in mosques and colleges (madrasas) in Iran and in its sphere of influence.[18-20]

Mosques and madrasas

The depleted remains of the mosques and madrasas of the Timurids, built by architects and craftsmen pressed into Timur's service from all over his conquests, reveal the influence of their predecessors in distribution and form. The predominant four-iwan plan imposed a symmetry ubiquitous since the Seljuks, but the gigantic scale of the Bibi Khanum mosque in Samarkand, like that of the palace at Kish, is Timur's own.[21-22] The later Timurids hardly matched the scale, though the builders of the Kalyani mosque at Bukhara tried.[23] Apart from the renovation of existing mosques, in fact Timur's successors paid more attention to providing facilities for worship in the context of the madrasa, and greater size was acquired by this type too, in whole and in part. The four-iwan form was the norm. The most notable

21 **Samarkand, Bibi Khanum mosque** begun 1399.
The ruins of the vast entrance iwan – 18 metres (59 feet)
wide and over 30 metres (100 feet) high – still dominate
much of Samarkand. The Spanish ambassador, Gonzales
de Clavijo, records that Timur had it rebuilt because the
original design was not high enough. The scale was
anticipated c. 1320 in the Friday mosque of the Taj al-Din
Ali Shah Jilan Tabrizi, vizier to Ilkhanid rulers Oljeitu and
Abu Said.

Bibi Khanum was Timur's mother-in-law, but Clavijo's
record implies that the mosque that bears her name was
founded by Timur himself as the Friday mosque (for
congregational prayer on the Muslim holy day) of his
capital. The court – 60 by 90 metres (197 by 295 feet) –
has four iwans, the main one on the qibla (the axis of
prayer towards Mecca) only marginally smaller than the
entrance and like it flanked by minarets rising from the
ground, as was the Timurid norm. Rebuilding to an
enhanced scale is suggested by the disparity between
the qibla frontispiece and the sanctuary dome behind it.
In distinction, the subsidiary axial chambers have no
frontispieces and ribbed domes. The current comprehensive
restoration and rebuilding programme involves much
retiling. Gigantism extended to experiments with domed

spaces too: ultimately descending from the kiosk mosque type (see volume 6, FOUR CALIPHATES, page 127), these usually concentrated on the isolated sanctuary, but in the Blue Mosque of Tabriz (1465) a great dome was thrown over what would normally have been the open court.

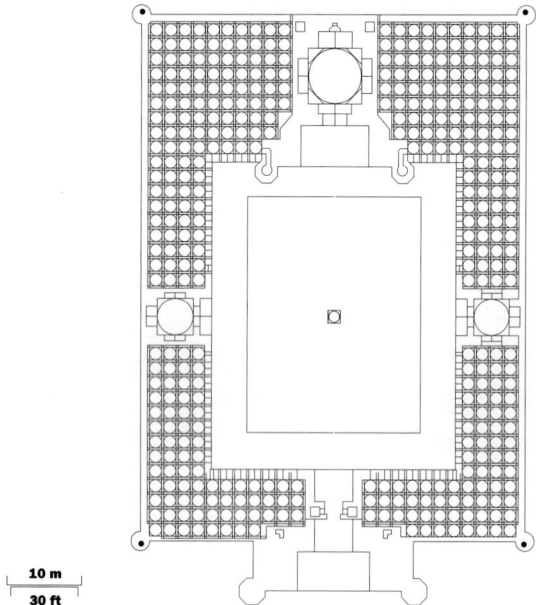

10 m
30 ft

22 **Samarkand, Bibi Khanum mosque** plan.

23 **Bukhara, Kalyani mosque** 1514, court towards qibla.

24 OVERLEAF **Samarkand, Registan** view with the much restored madrasas of Ulugh Beg (1417, left), Shir Dar (1619, right) and Tila Kari (1660, centre).

As elsewhere (Bukhara, for example), such impressive clustering results from royal patrons emulating their predecessors.

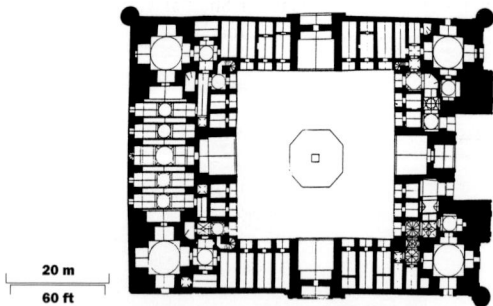

25 **Samarkand, Registan, Ulugh Beg madrasa** plan.

In the manner now typical of the Timurids, the generous entrance iwan occupies most of the front of Ulugh Beg's madrasa, but the minarets are detached at the corners and were presumably meant to be echoed at the back. Smaller iwans, flanked by cells behind a single grand arcade, address the court on its main axes. Beyond the qibla iwan, the mosque is an elongated hall communicating with a pair of cruciform domed chambers. Similar chambers fill the outer corners and these, at least, were probably meant to carry ribbed domes like the Shir Dar madrasa opposite.

examples were built for Gauhar Shad at Herat and Ulugh Beg on the Registan at Samarkand.[24-25]

As the buildings on the Registan demonstrate, mosques and madrasas are often difficult to distinguish until the interior is penetrated: then, of course, the complex prayer, teaching and residential requirements of the madrasa are apparent – as is the ingenuity of their planners in distributing their essential elements, particularly the collegiate mosque. Unless the site dictated entry from the west,[26] this could be an increasingly prominent qubba[27] with an iwan frontispiece in the centre of the western range of cells. On one level originally, increasing size led more often to student accommodation on several storeys.

After the Bibi Khanum example, frontispieces framing entrances generally screened most of the façade and were flanked by minarets rising from the ground. Domes tended to be bulbous and obscured by a frontispiece despite enhanced drums. Muqarnas – a honeycomb-like web formed from squinches – proliferate in arches (after the Isfahan Friday mosque, see volume 6, FOUR CALIPHATES, pages 134–35), in addition to interlaced ribs developing net-like zones of transition after the Ishrat Khaneh (see 15, pages 32–33). Far

26 **Samarkand, Registan, Shir Dar madrasa** court.
Built by the Shahibanid rulers of Transoxiana early in the
17th century opposite Ulugh Beg's madrasa on the eastern
side of the Registan, the pair of side domes here are more
assertive. The qibla dictated the siting of the mosque in the
western entrance wing, where it is balanced by a lecture
room. The student accommodation is arranged behind two
superimposed arcades.

27 **Samarkand, Registan, Tila Kari mosque and
madrasa** interior of qibla qubba.

more surfaces than heretofore are covered with geo-metrical or floral patterns in predominantly blue-glazed tiles. Yet the decorative use of structural form notwithstanding, colour and pattern are increasingly subject to, and reinforce, structural lines – unlike the jagged pattern which ramps over the exposed surfaces of the Gir-i Amir (see 14, page 31).

The tradition of the four-iwan mosque, established at Isfahan under the Seljuks, reached its high point there 500 years later under the Safavids. So too did the similar madrasa. Avoiding the rectangular junction of corridors between student cells, the latter develop a late Timurid tendency to penetrate chamfered corners of the court on the diagonals and provide direct access to lecture rooms. The supreme

28 Isfahan, Madrasa-yi Madar-i Shah 1706–15, qibla qubba and neighbouring cells.

Precedents for both the dominance of the mosque in the centre of the qibla range and the diagonal penetration of the corners from the court may be found outside the Safavid domains in Transoxiana: the former in the early 17th-century Tila Kari madrasa on the Registan in Samarkand, the latter in the Mir-i Arab madrasa at Bukhara of 1535.

example, with the collegiate mosque dominant in the centre of the range defining the direction of prayer (qibla) towards Mecca, is the Isfahan Madrasa-yi Madar-i Shah.[28]

This magnificent early 18th-century work represents the last flowering of an exceptionally rich tradition which produced or renovated and extended many mosques. The apogee was reached in the two main mosques of Shah Abbas I's Isfahan: the Sheikh Lutfullah and the Masjid-i Shah, which must surely rate among the most beautiful buildings in world.

Opposite the entrance to the palace, the domed Lutfullah was the palatine mosque.[29-31] At the southern end of the maidan, the Masjid-i Shah was the congregational mosque of the new capital.[32-36] As the maidan and the qibla were at an acute angle to one another, considerable virtue was made of necessity in bending the line of access to the axis of prayer in each building: privacy was enhanced by the circuitous corridor to the Sheikh Lutfullah's one great domed chamber. So too was drama – and withholding the impact of the Masjid-i Shah's sublime court until after penetration is a *coup de théâtre* of the first magnitude. In a singular aureole of unexcelled internal splendour on

29 **Isfahan, Sheikh Lutfullah mosque** c. 1600, plan.
Entered from the centre of a recess in the cloister
surrounding the maidan, a corridor skirts the north-west
and north-east sides of the domed qubba to the main portal
on the qibla opposite the mihrab (prayer niche).

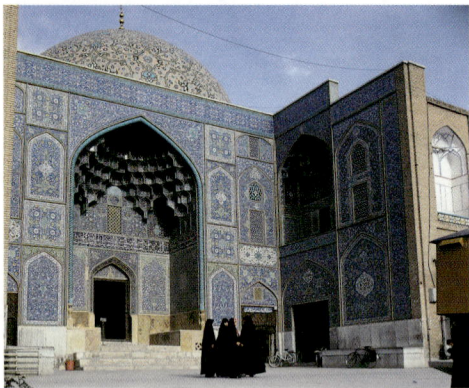

30 **Isfahan, Sheikh Lutfullah mosque** entrance from
the maidan.

   The portal is inscribed with a date corresponding to
1602 (presumably post-dating foundation by several
years), the interior with another corresponding to 1618.
The latter identifies the architect as the Isfahani ustad
(master) Muhammad Riza ibn Ustad Husein.

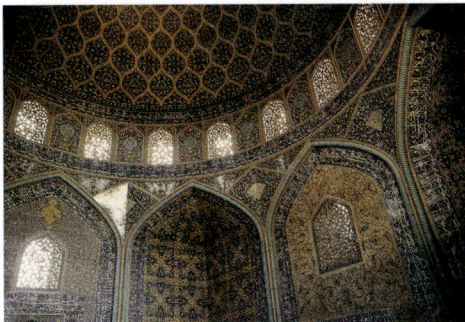

31 **Isfahan, Sheikh Lutfullah mosque** interior.

The domed octagon – 76 metres (250 feet) square – is
elementary in form but complex in surface pattern. Within
and between the pointed arches, the squinches have simple
grooved vaults (rather than muqarnas like the sumptuous
front entrance iwan, for instance) but are inlaid with mosaic
tiles in contrast to the painted tiles of dado and wall. The
arches are rimmed with a spiral moulding in turquoise but
their strength is reinforced by bands of deep blue with white
inscriptions. Like the empyraean at the rising and setting of
the sun, the dome dissolves in a cascade of blue and gold.

56

32 PREVIOUS PAGES **Isfahan, Masjid-i Shah** begun 1611.

An inscription on the portal is dated with the equivalent of 1616. Attributed to Ustad Abu'l Qasi, the building seems to have taken nearly 30 years to complete, thanks in part to suspension of work for several years to allow for settlement prior to tiling.

North facing and recessed beyond the line of the maidan cloisters, the entrance leads to a small domed vestibule and then into the triangular apse of an iwan which effects alignment through 45 degrees with the qibla. Across the huge four-iwan court, with side qubbas, as in the Samarkand Bibi Khanum mosque, the qibla qubba is flanked by twin prayer halls of eight domed bays each. These in turn are flanked by twin (non-residential) madrasas to the depth of the side iwans and their qubbas.

Complexity of form is avoided: muqarnas enliven the entrance, where the sun rarely illuminates the tilework, but elsewhere grooved semi-domes effect transition from square to circle – sometimes superimposed with decreasing depth to form lattice vaults. However, every surface is revetted with painted tiles except for the domes, which have moulded mosaics. Blue predominates, but it is graded in depth to assert structure or dissolve void.

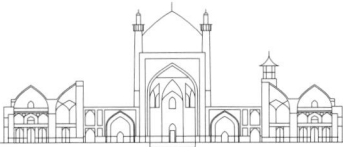

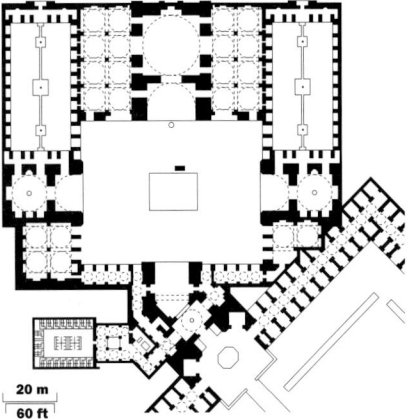

33 **Isfahan, Masjid-i Shah** section and plan.

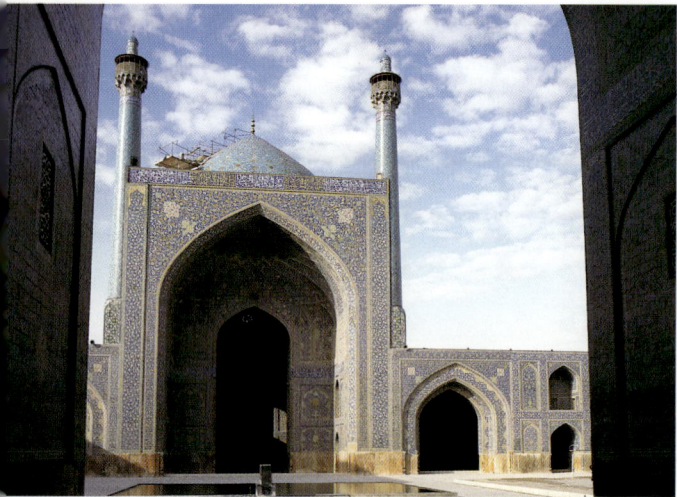

34 **Isfahan, Masjid-i Shah** qibla qubba.

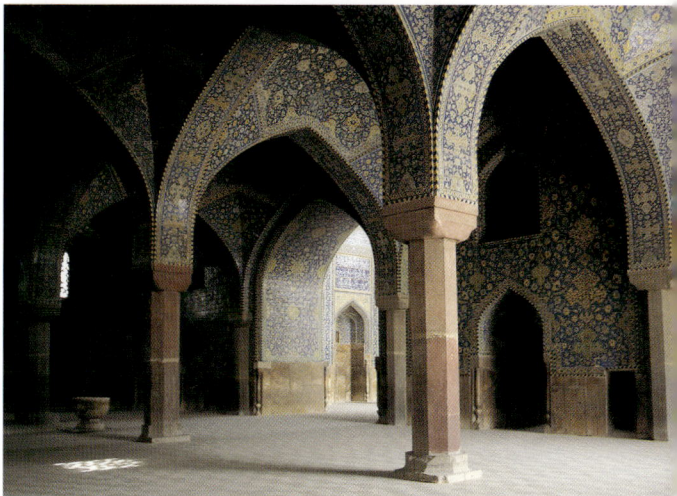

35 **Isfahan, Masjid-i Shah** view through southern prayer
hall to mihrab in qibla qubba.

the one hand, in a scenographic spectacle of open and closed forms, consistent in shape and material, ever changing in size, colour and pattern on the other, the ancient Iranian kiosk and the four-iwan court mosque types here achieve their apotheosis.

36 **Isfahan, Masjid-i Shah** qibla qubba interior.

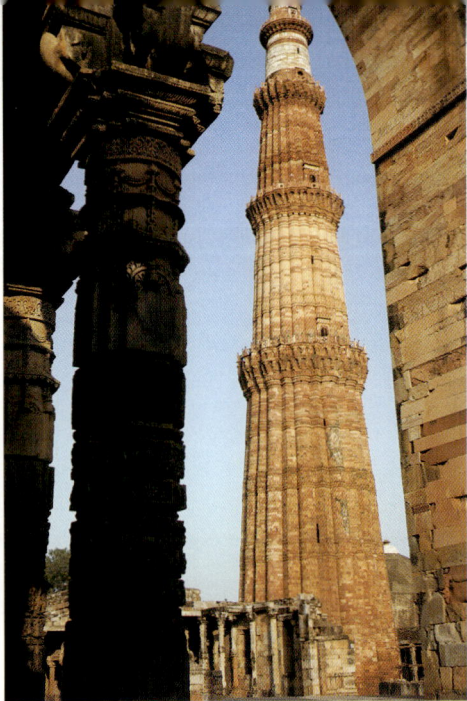

India here is used in its traditional sense to refer to the sub-continent now occupied by India, Pakistan and Bangladesh. If this section is exceptionally long, that is because India is exceptional: exceptional in the number of rich and powerful states which rose and fell there; exceptional in the number and splendour of their buildings; exceptional in the number and significance of those buildings still extant.

Following the example of Mahmud of Ghazni, who led his people in a series of raids on the major religious centres of northern India in the first three decades of the 11th century, Muhammad of Ghuri led his Afghan forces into India with much more determined purpose towards the end of the 12th century. Incessantly playing at war with one another, the Rajputs who had divided the north-west of the sub-continent were no match for the better equipped, flexible, grimly determined Muslims, and an extensive domain centred on modern Delhi was annexed to Ghuri in the early 1190s. On Muhammad's assassination in 1206, his commander in Delhi, Qtub ud-Din Aibek (once a

37 **Delhi, Quwwat al-Islam** detail of reused Hindu column in prayer hall and view of the Qtub minar, 1199.

Turkish slave), seized the initiative and founded the Mamluk dynasty of Delhi sultans. A signal display of proselytising militancy – comparable only to that of the 7th-century Arabs in north Africa – carried them right across India to Bengal within a couple of years, reducing venerable Hindu kingdoms to provinces.

Harried by the Mongols, prey to internal dissension, the Turkish Mamluks lost their Delhi throne to the Afghan Ala ud-Din Khalji in 1286. He took the sultanate to its peak with the conquest of the rich Hindu kingdoms of the west, centre and south. His inadequate successor was despatched in 1320 by Ghiyas ud-Din Tughluq, the governor of the Punjab, who was murdered five years later by his son, Muhammad. In an exercise of extraordinary brutality, the capital and its population were moved to the Deccani fortress of Devagiri (renamed Daulatabad), the better to hold a sub-continental empire. The exercise failed: the north revolted, the capital (and its population) moved back, the deranged sultan died in 1351 and the Deccan was taken by the Persian Bahamanis, who founded another sultanate centred on Gulbarga. Under Muhammad's cousin Firoz Shah, the Tughluqs held Delhi until Timur destroyed them – and much of the city – in 1398.

Buildings of the Delhi sultanate

The Turks of Ghazni had marked their triumph with
ceremonial minars. Penetrating India, the Ghurids
marked the triumph of Islam in the sub-continent with
the Quwwat al-Islam in Delhi, a mosque built of materials pillaged from Hindu temples dominated by a
declamatory iwan and the greatest of all ceremonial
minars.[37-40]

After an extensive phase of pillaging Hindu temples
for hypostyle prayer halls, the architects of Qtub ud-
din Aibek's various Afghan and Turkish successors
pressed local craftsmen into translating Iranian types
into Indian terms. Greatly extended by subsequent
rulers, the Quwwat al-Islam itself was the scene of
transition from indigenous to imported constructional
techniques. In the medium of plastered rubble, mosque
architecture ultimately went beyond the derivative
form of works such as Delhi's Begampuri[41] to explore
new depths of complexity at nearby Khirki[42] and
Nizam-ud-Din.[43] The experiments were not successful: in association with a novel form of madrasa, there
was a return to the traditional courtyard mosque type
in the funerary complex of Firoz Shah at Hauz Khas.

Before his translation from the Punjab to Delhi in

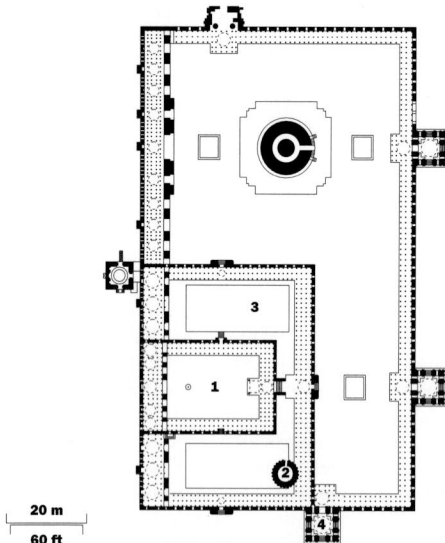

20 m
60 ft

38 **Delhi, Quwwat al-Islam** 1191 and later, plan.
(1) Original court and prayer hall; (2) Qtub minar;
(3) extensions of Iltutmish; (4) extensions of Ala ud-Din
Khalji and Alai Darwaza.

When the Turkish invaders occupied Delhi in 1191, garrisoning the fort of Rai Pithora at Lalkot (the seat of the Chahamana Rajputs) under the Amir Qtub ud-Din Aibek, the Hindu temples were demolished and their materials used in the construction of the great mosque built to celebrate the might of Islam. This, the first imperious monument of Muslim India (and a similar one at Ajmer), followed the plan of the first mosque of Islam, but the Hindu masons reused Hindu materials and followed their own structural and decorative traditions.

The extended platform of the main Hindu temple provides the court – the celebrated Gupta iron pillar, at least, remaining in situ. In the improvisation of the hypostyle prayer hall and colonnades, the lavishly carved (and presumably plastered) Hindu columns were superimposed to raise the reused ceilings to greater height than they would have had originally. A façade of five corbelled ogee arches was imposed to screen the trabeated prayer hall, but the qibla iwan rises higher than the superimposed piers behind. The Hindu masons, unfamiliar with the true voussoir arch, recall the horseshoe forms of their ancient tradition and bands of progenitive lotus mouldings (padma), like those in the jambs of temple portals, are flanked by bands of Islamic calligraphy. The second sultan, Iltutmish (1211–36) extended the prayer-hall screen by three bays on either end, enclosed the additional courts before them (the southern one incorporating the great minar), and projected his lavishly incised octagonal tomb from the south-east corner.

After the specific precedents set at Ghazni and Jam (see volume 6, FOUR CALIPHATES, page 184), but in accordance with a tradition in India that may be traced back to the Mauryan pillars of the law (see volume 5, INDIA AND SOUTH-EAST ASIA, page 31), Qtub raised his great minar in commemoration of the triumph of his Muslim order (see 37, page 64). Of red sandstone and grey quartzose, this is circular in plan with a variety of circular and acute-angled projections. Originally there were three storeys marked by balconies on muqarnas and ringed by bands of Islamic calligraphy and Hindu foliage.

A century after its foundation, the great mosque was further extended by Sultan Ala ud-Din Khalji (1286–1316). This involved the doubling of the prayer hall behind a taller arcade, the erection of new colonnades along the other three sides of a court nearly four times the area covered by Iltutmish, and the provision of four monumental entrance pavilions and a minar twice the size of Qtub's.

39 **Delhi, Quwwat al-Islam** view from court to
prayer hall.

40 **Delhi, Quwwat al-Islam** Alai Darwaza, 1311.

Of Ala ud-Din's grandiose plans, only the southern
entrance pavilion – the first of a long series of monuments
executed in the strikingly contrasted red sandstone and
white marble – reached any degree of completeness.
Over a figured base into which steps are cut, this is a
qubba, self-contained like its Zoroastrian or Roman
triumphal antecedents despite its projected integration
with the southern colonnade. Divided into two registers
of screened arched windows and blind panels, the east,
south and west façades are each dominated by a double-
voussoir arch springing from colonnettes and relieved
along the intrados by the spearhead valance that was to
be so characteristic of the works of the later sultanate.
The north façade is not articulated but its arch is treated
to elaborately beaded mouldings worthy of the fertile
imagination of a Rajastani. Interior and exterior are
profusely ornamented with low-relief carving including
calligraphic bands. The qubba, lit by only the innermost
windows, has five receding arches forming squinches to
support a true dome. This small work was to provide a
major prototype for sultanate tombs.

41 **Delhi, Begampuri mosque** c. 1350, court.

On a high platform, the court is bordered by prayer hall
and cloisters, as usual, but no longer of pillaged materials
these are formed of arcaded bays with shallow domes
carried on pendentives over simple paired piers. The qibla is
marked by a great iwan. Built of coarse plastered masonry,
there are traces of glazed tiling which once presumably
sheathed all exposed surfaces. The battered minarets
attached to the frontispiece (as in contemporary Iran)
produce an idiosyncratic pylon-like form.

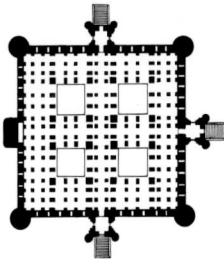

42 **Delhi, Khirki mosque** c. 1375, plan.

The vizier of Sultan Firoz Shah (1351–85), Khan-Jahan
i-Tilangani, built three mosques in Delhi experimenting
with the extension of cover at the expense of the court.
The most advanced is the one at Khirki: perfectly formal
in its symmetry about the cardinal axes, the three ranges
of triple arcades (riwaks) along all four sides and across
the centre frame four square internal courts. With entrance
pavilions on the south, north and east, a projection behind
the mihrab to the west and tapering turrets at most
corners, the absence of any dominant feature on the skyline
reinforced the impression of homogeneity. It was this
quality, however, that made the approach unworkable: it
denied authority to the qibla and it is unsurprising that the
experiments were not sustained.

43 Delhi, Nizam-ud-Din, Kalan mosque c. 1370, arcades.

As at Khirki, the Kalan mosque has four courts, but they are bordered by a single range of arcades to all sides except the west (before the qibla), where there are three ranges. Stout battered walls of plastered rubble pierced by relatively small screened windows give the appearance of rugged strength.

44 OVERLEAF **Multan, tomb of Rukn-i-Alam** c. 1320.

Commander of the sultanate's frontier forces based at
Multan in the Punjab, Ghiyas ud-Din Tughluq built one
of the most magnificent tombs of the entire Muslim world.
It was apparently first meant for himself, but after he seized
the sultanate in 1320 he assigned it to the sufi Sheikh
Rukn-i-Alam. Multan maintained direct ties with Iran,
whose brick and tile tradition was well adapted to the
conditions of the Indus plains, and the influence of the tomb
of Oljeitu at Sultaniya (see volume 6, FOUR CALIPHATES,
pages 145–47) is obvious. Further, the Saminids of Bukhara
seem to be recalled by the domed turrets at the corners.
There was also a local tradition of tomb-building which
provided the steeply battered walls, octagonal clerestory
and broad dome. In addition to inlaid blue tiles – used
sparingly in bands around the lower storey, more lavishly
on the pilasters, frieze and clerestory window frames and
to relieve the base of the great white dome – patterned
brickwork and carved timber play important roles.

45 **Delhi, Tughluqabad, tomb of Ghiyas ud-Din Tughluq** c. 1325.

In Delhi Ghiyas ud-Din Tughluq founded a new capital guarded by a stoutly walled citadel. His mausoleum combines the military might imported from Multan with the elegance of Ala ud-Din's Alai Darwaza (see 40, page 73).

46 **Delhi, Nizam-ud-Din, tomb of Khan-Jahan i-Tilangani** 1369.

An expansion of the canopy form (the Indian chattri) on the precedent of the Dome of the Rock in Jerusalem, the dome rests on eight arcades and is surrounded by a gallery with a saucer dome over the central bay of each side.

47 **Delhi, Kotla Firoz Shah** reconstruction (after Brown).

Like most of its predecessors, Firoz Shah's new seat was
protected by a citadel integrated with town defences. There
are considerable denuded remains of the fort palace on an
extensive terrace beside the Yamuna river. Incorporating all
the constituent elements of the earliest Indian palaces,
themselves derived from the Achaemenids, Kotla Firoz Shah
lacks the formality and, indeed, the great vaulted structures
of Abbasid or Ghaznavid complexes. Instead, trabeated
pavilions of a type by no means unfamiliar in India seem to
have been distributed in a way which recalls the tent palaces
of central Asia, for which the Tughluqs' Turkish ancestors
must have felt as much affinity. Here too, most significantly,
an ancient Indian form plays a major symbolic role: a
prasada apparently once complete with chattris on its
terraces was built to support a pillar of the law credited to
the Mauryan emperor Ashoka (c. 270–232 BC), which Firoz
removed to the capital from Tapra.

Within the massive battered battlements, beyond the
main western gate and its stout barbican, was a vast
irregular enclosure before the principal mosque. Through
the enclosure, a circuitous route led to the sultan's quarters
(Daulat Khana), with the court of public audience (Diwan-i-
Am) dominated by a talar on its southern side, the private

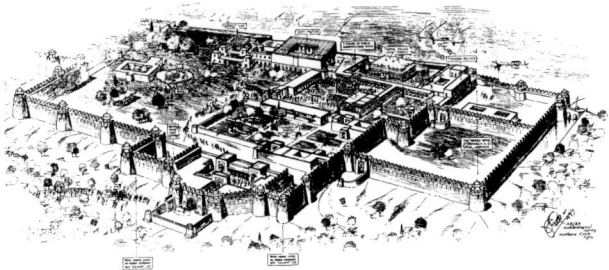

royal court (Diwan-i-Khas) on a riverside terrace beyond
this to the east next to the mosque, and the harem quarters
to its south.

The new capital is reputed to have had eight large
mosques, but little remains even of the principal Friday
mosque within the fort: conventional in plan with
colonnades around the court, only its north entrance
pavilion and the qibla wall survive. Connected with it
on the north is the celebrated and well-preserved stepped
prasada-like structure erected as the platform for the
Mauryan pillar.

1320, Ghiyas ud-Din Tughluq had taken the imported funerary tradition to new heights in the tomb of Sheikh Rukn-i-Alam at Multan.[44] There and in Delhi, at once derivative and idiosyncratic, the rulers of the sultanate laid the foundations of the greatest funerary tradition of the Islamic world[45–46] And on the basis of several centuries of development, largely lost to us now, they set the pattern for the Mughal palace.[47]

The end of the sultanate

Following Muhammad Tughluq's retreat from Daulatabad in 1338, the governor of the Deccan declared his independence as Bahaman Shah: he moved the capital from Daulatabad to Gulbarga and it was moved again in 1429 to Bidar. About the middle of the 14th century too, the governor of Bengal declared himself sultan: he moved from the old Hindu seat at Gaur to nearby Hazrat Pandua. Kashmir followed. After Timur's destruction of the Tughluqs in 1398, there was a spate of secessions: Malik Sarwar founded the Sharqi (eastern) sultanate of Jaunpur in 1394; Dilawar Ghuri established himself in Malwa in 1401 and his successor Hoshang Shah founded a magnificent new capital at Mandu; Ahmad Shah made

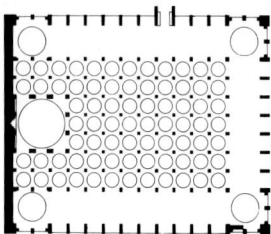

48 Gulbarga, Friday mosque 1367, plan.

Like the slightly later Delhi works of Tilangani (see 42–43, pages 75–76), the approach here reflects an interest in the multi-bay prayer halls of the Friday mosque of Isfahan. On a rectangular base, arcades two bays deep and a triple-aisled prayer hall may be distinguished, but the minor domed bays of the hall are extended to cover the whole court area and the cloisters are cross-spanned by great single ogee arches springing from low imposts on simple square piers between secondary domed spaces at each corner. Purely architectonic, the entire visual effect is drawn from the simple repetition of the two types of arch, which seem to float over anonymous supports. In subtle counterpoint, cusped arches make an appearance in the northern entrance, and the mihrab and squinches of the qubba have an idiosyncratic trefoil form.

49 **Gulbarga, Friday mosque** outer arcades.

The low-sprung, broad-span ogee arch which gives the Gulbarga mosque its special character was not to be widely used by the later Bahamanis and their Barid successors. They favoured more conventionally proportioned forms without imposts, as in the Bidar Friday mosque.

50 **Gulbarga, Friday mosque** inner arcades and mihrab.

51 **Bidar Mahmud Gawan madrasa** c. 1470.

Bidar was founded as the Deccani capital after Ahmad Shah I seized the throne from his brother in 1429. Apart from its spectacular fortress, its chief claim to architectural distinction is the great, formal four-iwan madrasa of Mahmud Gawan, the Persian minister of Muhammad Shah III (1463–82). Despite the quality of the work, the type represented by this Iranian importation was not to be favoured in India except for its bulbous form of dome.

An elevation of three storeys of cells for students is rare, but the rigorously symmetrical four-iwan plan of Mahmud Gawan's foundation, its arcading and its revetment of brilliantly coloured tiles are related to contemporary Timurid work, the most notable intermediary between Gawan's building and the great foundation of Samarkand being the lost madrasa of Gauhar Shad at Herat. As in several Timurid madrasas, the Bidar work's mosque is balanced by a hall on the other side of the entrance. The monumental minarets of the eastern front are exceptional among the works of the Bahamanis. The bulbous form of dome – as yet squatter than the Timurid norm – appears here for the first important time in India. It was to predominate the 16th century.

52 **Jaunpur, Atala mosque** prayer-hall frontispiece.

Jaunpur was established by Sultan Firoz Shah in 1358 on an ancient Hindu site by the river Gumti. The most prominent of all the city's mosques – Firoz Shah's own foundation, the great Atala mosque – takes its departure from the Begampuri type (see 41, page 74). Its greater monumentality derives not only from the adjustment of the proportions of the main elements, but from the substitution for rubble of fine grey sandstone and granite won from temples or dressed specifically for them by Hindu masons, whose names are cut into the fabric.

With double-height colonnades in place of the Begampuri's arcades for the cloisters and prayer hall, the Atala mosque's most extraordinary feature is the set of pylon-like iwan frontispieces masking the principal and subsidiary qubbas of the prayer hall. With screened arch and trabeated portal, these are even more exaggerated in height than in the Begampuri and formidable battered towers replace the tapering turret-like minars. The precedent set by the Atala mosque was followed for the Lal Darwaza and Friday mosque, the latter larger at least in its parts.

himself sultan of Gujarat with his capital at Ahmedabad in 1411. And following the usual period of pillaging Hindu temples, distinct architectural traditions developed in all these states, either in accordance with the imported proclivites of their immigrant rulers or on the basis of a rich indigenous legacy – or, indeed, from the cross-fertilisation of the two. The former was the case in the Bahamani kingdom,[48-51] Jaunpur[52] and Malwa.[53-58] The indigenous tradition was still virile in Bengal, Kashmir and Gujarat and the grafting of imported forms on to it had spectacular results.[59-63]

In Delhi the Tughluqs were replaced by Timur's

53–54 FOLLOWING PAGES **Mandu, Friday mosque** entrance front from Ashrafi Mahal portico and hall of public audience (so-called Hindola Mahal).

The Tughluq governors of Malwa ruled from Dhar and the first sultan stayed there. The second Ghuri ruler, Hoshang Shah (1405–35), chose the virtually impregnable plateau of Mandu some 35 kilometres (22 miles) from Dhar as the site for a new capital. This had been a seat of the Hindu Paramaras and Hoshang Shah built his own royal complex on that of the Hindus around the Munja tank.

The earliest Malwan mosques were largely assembled

from materials pillaged from Hindu temples. However, able to attract the artisans of Delhi underemployed by the successors of Firoz Shah, Hoshang Shah was not content with mere improvisation. The prayer hall of the great mosque is of the open hypostyle type – common among the contemporary works of neighbouring Gujarat but rare in the sultanate – yet the austerity of Firozian forms is preferred to Gujarati floridity. It dispenses with Hindu structure in favour of an extended series of identical domed bays, interrupted before the qibla by three nine-bay qubbas – but no iwan or frontispiece – and by a monumental entrance pavilion in the centre of the east range. Domed turrets mark the corners, as in the mosques of Tilangani. The piers are those of Firozian Delhi but the arches retain the ogee profile also favoured in the Deccan and decorative play is made with flying arches, after the non-structural principle of the native tradition but with Firozian restraint in practice. The remaining elements of the principal palace complex are dominated by Hoshang Shah's great audience pavilion, the Hindola Mahal (c. 1425). Recalling precedents stretching back to the Sassanians through the winter prayer hall of the Isfahani Friday mosque and the Baghdad Ortmah han, the great room is dominated by huge transverse ogee arches which once carried a timber-beamed roof.

55 **Mandu, Friday mosque** Ashrafi Mahal.

A fine ceremonial way led from Mandu's Delhi gate past the walled royal enclosure to the cult centre. Here the crossing of a subsidiary axis, extending the qibla of the Friday mosque, aligned the tomb of Hoshang Shah to the west and, to the east, the Ashrafi Mahal – one of India's earliest formally planned madrasas.

Little but the base remains. The open court of the original madrasa seems to have been filled to provide the foundation for the tomb chamber of Mahmud i-Khalji. One of the corner pavilions of the original structure, too, provided the base for a seven-storey tower of victory.

56 **Mandu, Friday mosque** tomb of Hoshang Shah.
Among the earliest Muslim buildings in India to be entirely sheeted in white marble, Hoshang Shah's weighty qubba is a revision of the sultanate type represented by the tomb of Ghiyas ud-Din Tughluq.

57 **Mandu, palace** sultan's apartments (Daulat Khana).
   The private apartments and harems built around the
Munja tank by later rulers are typical of the secular
structures of the period. Iwans address courts in the Daulat
Khana, below a pillared pavilion for private audience
overlooking the lake from the top terrace.

58 **Mandu, palace** harem wing (so-called Jahaz Mahal).

The indigenous prasada is most persuasively recalled in the airy balconies and kiosk-crowned pavilion projecting into the lake from the harem's so-called Ship Palace, but the effect depended upon a revetment of glazed tiles. Brought to Mandu from Multan, tilemaking flourished in the Malwan capital throughout the 15th century and its subtle turquoise and radiant yellow were never surpassed.

nominee, but his undistinguished Sayyid line did little
more than sustain itself in the capital until despatched
by more Afghans under Bahlol Lodi in 1451. Iskandar
Lodi (1488–1516) managed to re-assemble something
of an empire in north India, with its capital at Agra,
and his reign has left some considerable monuments.[64]
His grandiloquent son alienated his main supporters.
They appealed to the Timurid prince Babur who, dispossessed of his inheritance in central Asia but forging
a kingdom in Afghanistan, responded in the recognition of a great opportunity. He despatched the Lodi
sultan in 1526 and occupied Agra.

59 **Gaur, unidentified tomb** early 15th century.
    At least until the 16th century, Bengal's Muslim builders
– like the Hindus before them – generally referred to the
local vernacular for the great majority of their works: the
mud and bamboo hut with its curved roof (bangaldar)
was still the ultimate prototype. Below the cornice,
which follows the curve of the low-pitched roof, walls
are consistently relieved by recessed panels in a rectilinear
framework recalling the timber reinforcement of mud walls.
Minarets are added at the corners. Tombs are usually square
and the burial chamber rising above the curved roof may

have a dome. The mosques conforming to the type are
invariably rectangular, usually of two or three ranges of five
arcaded and individually domed bays, but empty repetition
often produced as many as ten or twelve.

60 **Srinagar, Shah Hamadan mosque** c. 1400.

Imported forms were less common in Kashmir than
the pragmatic timber one modelled on the ubiquitous
village shrine – a simple square timber structure, usually
with verandahs or balconies projecting more or less
symmetrically, surmounted by a pyramidal roof and spire-
like minaret.

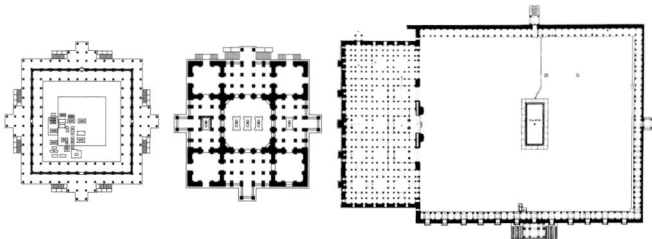

61 **Ahmedabad, Friday mosque** 1423, plan with tombs of Ahmad Shah (centre) and his queens (left).

Ahmedabad was founded as the capital of Gujarat on a Solanki site. Theory notwithstanding, in practice few Indian cities were decidedly formal in plan, but here a great axial thoroughfare, spanned by a magnificent triumphal arch, linked the citadel with the Friday mosque, itself aligned with the tombs of the ruler and his wives.

62 **Ahmedabad, Friday mosque** prayer hall.

Like the majority of the mosques of the new capital, the main one developed the arcaded screen type popular in Delhi, with Hindu pillars – or pillars produced by Hindu craftsmen – visible through the arcades. The slightly projecting frontispiece incorporates minarets which rise from the ground, as in contemporary Timurid Iran, but they are applied to the outer face and their bases have much of the complexity of Solanki piers.

In the unsurpassed Friday mosque, with five large chambers to its prayer hall, the arcaded façade screens only the three central zones. There is a clear progression in height from the trabeated outer bays to the arcaded intermediate ones and on to the great central frontispiece with its Solanki-inspired piers and gorgeous screened windows. This responds to an increasing number of superimposed galleries within, the central chamber with its flying arches rivalling the great open halls of the Jains.

Ahmad Shah's tomb, of the canopy type but square in plan, has deep screened colonnades leading from porches at the cardinal points to the main tomb chamber, whose great corbelled vault rests somewhat haphazardly on beams extended between pilasters in the arcaded walls. The queens' tomb (Rani-ka Huira) is a raised open

court surrounded by doubled colonnades with screens
supported on the central range of pillars. These works
inspired many others over the century and a half of the
sultanate's independent existence.

63 Ahmedabad, mortuary complex of Rani Rupvati
1505.

Ahmedabad is particularly notable for its mortuary complexes (rauzas) in which tomb and mosque confront one another across an open court. Matching in exquisitely refined detail, the former usually conforms to the model provided by the tomb of Ahmad Shah, the latter, naturally, is of the old unscreened type. For want of a frontispiece to the prayer hall, minarets were applied to the front corners, but tending there to deny the composition integrity they were progressively reduced in scale until they became mere ornamental turrets, as here. With this went the proliferation of subsidiary projections such as balconies.

64 **Delhi, Siri, Moth-ki mosque** early 16th century.

Rejecting the novel, satisfying but inappropriate centralised plan of the Khirki mosque (see 42, page 75), Lodi architects reverted to the arcaded prayer hall addressing an open court. Their experiments with centralisation in the design of the arcade culminated here: each bay is domed and though the arches are consistent in size and relief, the outer plane of the central one is raised with panelled piers to form an iwan frontispiece which interrupts the deep awning. The piers between the intermediate bays echo those of the frontispiece in a lower key and the whole composition is closed at the ends by broad piers pierced with elegant niches.

درختهای بنا ... هم هست کرد و کرد و حوض تمام کرده گذار

بای عمن بی چ عمین بست در وقت نزد آمدن بنا به بسیار

Babur retired from India as soon as possible to lay out gardens in Kabul.[65] He died in 1530, far from having consolidated his hold on India. His son Humayun made a good start in campaigns against Malwa and Gujarat but lost himself to indolence and his throne to the Afghan Sher Shah in 1540. After 15 years of exile in Iran (see 2, page 11), he won the throne back from Sher Shah's successor but died within the year. His son Akbar, born in exile and only 13 on his accession, survived to demonstrate his worth thanks to exceptionally able guardianship. Brusquely assuming the government on attaining his majority, he spent the next 40 years expanding his power with outstanding generalship and consolidating it with enlightened policies: the Rajputs were under control by 1568, Gujarat was absorbed by 1573, Bengal the following year, Kashmir in 1583, Orissa in 1592 and Sind in 1595.

In the Deccan the Bahamanis had succumbed to factional rivalry in 1538 and their empire had been divided between its viceroys into six states. They united against Vijayanagar to the south and destroyed it in 1565, but the conflict – and conflict between them-

65 **Babur inspecting a garden** (Mughal miniature).

selves – left them vulnerable to Akbar. Nevertheless, it
took his dynasty a century to overcome Bijapur and
Golconda, the two Deccani states which had won most
from Vijayanagar and whose rulers spent much of the
proceeds on embellishing their capitals in an increasingly florid style developed by grafting Hindu ornament on to Persian forms inherited from the
Bahamanis.[66–67]

Akbar constructed an exceptionally sound admin-
istrative edifice and cemented it by mollifying his
Hindu subjects. Authority in provincial administration was divided between the chief executive officer
and the revenue collector, and office-holders were
remunerated in cash rather than land. The Rajputs

66 **Bijapur, Friday mosque** 1565, prayer hall, plan and
section.

Standing on a high, galleried base, the Friday mosque of
Ali I (1557–80) has an open arcaded prayer hall whose outer
bays are extended to define the court. The qibla is asserted
by a great hemispherical dome on a square clerestory,
the latter richly arcaded and surmounted by merlons, the
former rising like a bud from an upturned lotus.

As at Gulbarga (see 49, page 86), the cool restraint of the

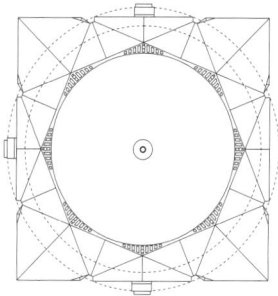

interior derives from the repetition of simple recessed
arcades springing low from plain rectangular piers. Lattice-
like interpenetrating arches (originally imported from Persia
by the Bahamanis) effect transition from square to circle or
octagon in the minor bays. In the main qubba this is most
spectacularly done by interlocking arches, rising from
rotated squares (as in the star-shaped plans of the Deccani
Hindus) and spanning between the corresponding piers of
the central bays in adjoining sides.

67 PREVIOUS PAGES **Bijapur, funerary complex of
Ibrahim II** 1626–33.

The tomb complexes of the Adil Shahi rulers usually
consist of a three- or five-bay mosque and a larger mortuary
pavilion with a double dome rising high above a lofty
verandah. The finest surviving example is that of Ibrahim II
(1580–1626) just outside the Mecca gate. On a rectangular
terrace set in a chahar bagh with a sumptuous entrance
pavilion, the mosque and tomb confront one another over
an ornamental pool with a fountain. Embellishment, much
of it distinctly Hindu in inspiration but not without
precedent in Bahamani work, includes prominent awnings
(chadyas) on rich corbelled brackets, cusps to distinguish
central arches, filigree balustrades, elegant chattris and
corner finial-like minarets with lotus and bud-like caps
which reflect the exaggeratedly bulbous form of the dome.

68 **Hyderabad, Char minar** 1592.

The convolution and multiplication of forms at variance
with the scale of the whole, characteristic of Deccani
architecture, is nowhere better illustrated than in the
celebrated Char minar which marks the crossing of the two
main axes of Hyderabad.

were left autonomous and invested with high office, army commands and imperial honours. Akbar himself married a Rajput bride who bore him his heir. His monarchy acquired an aura of sanctity derived from the ancient Vedic tradition and, indeed, his whole approach was symptomatic of his highly unorthodox attitude to Islam. He promulgated a new syncretic faith, the Din-Illahi, which acknowledged many theologies and to which the monarch was central. Apart from the imperial system itself, the most obvious expression of Akbar's syncretism was the synthesis in painting and architecture of Persian forms brought back and promoted with vigour by Humayun and those traditional in India.[68]

Akbar's legacy was one of the greatest empires the world had ever seen and his heirs were impressive. Jahangir (1605–27) was perhaps the least effective, yet expansion continued throughout his reign and he inherited his great-grandfather's taste for laying out gardens. Shah Jahan (1627–59) took the empire to its greatest height culturally, furthered the conquest of the south but was less successful abroad. The system of divided provincial authority had begun to break down, but partnership between Persian and Hindu was largely sustained until the ailing, ageing emperor was superseded and incarcerated by his son Aurangzeb (1659-1707). A zealous Muslim, he took the empire to its widest extent by completing the conquest of the south, but sowed the seeds of its destruction with his intolerance. His heir was the last impressive ruler, but short lived. His descendants were humiliated by the Persians, their provincial governors asserted independence in the time-honoured way and the resultant chaos favoured the intervention of foreigners, particularly the British.

The imperial mosque

Of several mosques built while the Mughals were establishing themselves, the Qila-i-Kuhna in Delhi's Purana Qila[69] is the most important. The prayer hall is distinguished in height, as in the Moth-ki mosque at Siri (see 64, page 109), and the centralisation of the façade through the manipulation of planes is at its most subtle. The greatest of the many mosques of Akbar's reign is Fatehpur Sikri's Badshahi ('imperial') mosque,[70] its traditional court plan dominated by the triumphal Buland Darwaza built to commemorate the conquest of Gujarat.[71] The prayer hall continues in the

69 Delhi, Purana Qila, Qila-i-Khuna mosque 1541.

The manipulation of façade planes is at its most subtle: the five arches progress in height from the sides to the centre but the elevated blind arcades are applied before each in counterpoint, the outer ones being taller but shallower than the intermediate ones and the central one taller still but deeper. The foremost plane of the frontispiece has a spearhead valance and this is echoed on the inner arches of the intermediate bays while the plain white marble surround of the innermost central arch echoes the blind outer arches of the side bays, both in the context of coloured inlay.

plane of the western cloister range but is distinguished
in height and centred on an iwan frontispiece and
qubba. Of red sandstone with coloured stone and
white marble inlay, again, its incorporation of decorative details from the native repertory is characteristic of Akbar's works.

Shah Jahan and his successor were prolific mosque
builders – Aurangzeb even notorious. The influence
of Persia is more pervasive than it had been under
Akbar, most notably in the splendid brick and tiled
mosque of Wazir Khan at Lahore.[72] At his apogee,
Shah Jahan's architects worked in coloured stone and
marble, combining native elements ranging from the
platform to the dome (chattri) with the imported
iwan and bulbous dome – as much Deccani as
Timurid in profile. The example set at Fatehpur Sikri

70 **Fatehpur Sikri, Badshahi mosque** 1570s, court and
Buland Darwaza.

Here the cloisters return along the western side in the
Persian manner, though their arcades mask a trabeated
structure beneath deep awnings and chattris. Heightened
and deepened and interrupted by a typical early Mughal
frontispiece but not breaking forward, they form a prayer

hall which contrasts markedly with the freestanding block of the Afghan period. The qibla qubba, its dome hidden by the frontispiece, is richly decorated within with carved, painted and inlaid ornament. Transition is effected by arched squinches rather than by corbelling as in the two subsidiary qubbas. In the qibla frontispiece, as in the eastern Badshahi ('imperial') gate, the only one to survive in its original form, the red sandstone used throughout the complex is eclipsed by coloured stone inlay.

71 Fatehpur Sikri, Badshahi mosque Buland Darwaza.

The triumphal Buland ('lofty') gate, bearing celebrated pantheistic inscriptions, replaced the south portal above the service quarters of the town to commemorate Akbar's subjection of Gujarat. It was to be seen rather than used. From within, the composition – incorporating stepped tiers bearing chattris to mask the back of the frontispiece – seems somewhat incongruous, but outside, its great iwan thrusts forwards resplendently over the most precipitous face of the plateau.

was followed in the Friday mosque at Delhi's Shahja-hanabad, but the venerable alternative of an open arcaded prayer hall, co-terminous with the qibla wall and without frontispiece or minarets, was also adopted for the superb white marble Mothi mosque in the fort at Agra.[73-74] But it was the Delhi work which provided the prototype for India's last great imperial mosques (and their many, increasingly decadent, followers).

72 PREVIOUS PAGES **Lahore, mosque of Wazir Khan** 1634, court.

The frontispiece stands out from the twin arcaded bays of the prayer hall, themselves significantly higher than the blind arcades around the other sides of the court, and minarets rise from all four corners. Cells behind the north, south and east ranges of blind arcades suggest that the mosque was also a madrasa. Contrary to Persian practice, variation from the base plane of the wall is provided by the blind arcades and its rectilinear framework. The dazzling effect of the exterior is derived from the brilliant Punjabi mosaic tilework in the framework of glazed red brick. Inside, the painted stucco, especially over the rich muqarnas, is equally brilliant.

73 **Agra, Mothi mosque** 1645, prayer hall from court.

Chattris are used instead of minarets on all four corners of the prayer hall, with smaller chattris between, and the three bulbous domes rise unobscured. In contrast to the cloisters in the Friday mosque at Delhi, all the arches are cusped and there is maximum consistency of form. As no sandstone is visible and black marble is used only for the calligraphy, nothing disturbs the work's cool elegance.

74 **Delhi, Shahjahanabad, Friday mosque** 1644, prayer
hall from court.

The Delhi mosque surpasses even the Fatehpur Sikri one
in extent. Like many of its Indian predecessors, and the
Agra Mothi mosque, it is raised on a platform surrounded
by arcades, but with rare concern for external effect the
platform is high enough for the arcades to be left open on
both sides without risk of pollution. Monumental flights of
steps ascend to the emperor's eastern entrance, inspired by
the Buland Darwaza, and to subsidiary ones for the public
north and south. To some extent this arrangement recalls
the four-iwan plan common in Iran after the Seljuks. As in
the Fatehpur Sikri mosque the cloisters return around the
western side, but the more elevated prayer hall is projected
into the court as a freestanding block as in the Qila-i-Kuhna
and its predecessors. As in many Timurid and Safavid
works, the frontispiece rises high above the five bays of each
wing to mask much of the great qibla qubba's dome. There
are no chadyas and chattris are used only on the entrance
pavilions, on the rear corners of the prayer hall – where they
stand in for the elegant minarets of the main façade – and
over slender miniature minarets applied to the sides of the
frontispiece in the Safavid manner. The mosque is built of
red sandstone, but the revetment of marble predominates.

The imperial palace

Babur was a man of acute aesthetic awareness, attuned to the sophisticated works of the Timurids and Safavids. In his memoirs he claims credit for several gardens and pavilions and betrays some contempt for the Indian tradition. One of the few Indian buildings he did admire was the palace of Man Singh at Gwalior (see volume 5, INDIA AND SOUTH-EAST ASIA, pages 181–82) – presumably because its architect, reducing the monumental to the exquisite, adapted the ubiquitous west Asian court and vaulted hall to suit a climate which Babur specifically deplored. Apart from the Ram and Zahara gardens at Agra – the former apparently centered on a hasht behisht – his major work was a columned portico there which no doubt conformed to the type most recently represented by Shah Tahmasp's chihil sutun at Qazvin, if it did not actually emulate the apadana-like Timurid structure the emperor himself had so admired in the Bagh-i-Maydan of Samarkand. Even had imported craftsmen been employed on the job, such a structure would hardly

75 Akbar holding court in an encampment outside a town (Mughal miniature).

have been much at variance with the form of audience
hall which, nearly two millennia earlier, the Indians
had derived from the same apadana prototype.[75]

The first great citadel built after the advent of the
Mughals, the Purna Qila which dominated
Humayun's new Delhi capital of Dinpannah, seems to
have followed the precedent set ready to hand by Firoz
Shah. Akbar furthered the tradition in his series of metropolitan and provincial fortresses, including most
notably those of Agra, Lahore and Allahabad. Beyond
their general distribution,[76] the defence work is the
most substantial legacy of Akbar's period in all his
greatest forts, but pronounced aesthetic sensibility
was brought to bear on the design of even the most
utilitarian elements, achieving a compromise between
oppressive power and festive display which is at its
most admirable, perhaps, at Agra.

The principal royal seat was clearly designed to
impress the native princes but also to win their admi-
ration. In a way utterly typical of the Din-Illahi, more-
over, much in the decorative scheme is of Islamic
inspiration but much else derives from the indigenous
tradition. Akbar's appreciation of the resources of
indigenous artisans is explicit in the official record of

76 **Agra, Red Fort** 1564–65, plan.

The Agra fort is an irregular semi-circle with its base parallel to the Yamuna river. On the river side there is a broad terrace between the two-tiered walls, breaking out into irregularly spaced bastions of which the most prominent commands a water gate. The main entrance is the Delhi gate to the west. Its barbican has a canted entrance forcing the line of approach up a steep, restricted ramp parallel to the walls and through three obtuse- and acute-angled turns.

77 Agra, Red Fort Jahangiri Mahal façade.

The Jahangiri Mahal's plan is symmetrical along the clearly defined central axis from the entrance with its striking coloured frontispiece, through the square central court to the recessed terrace overlooking the river. Something of the great caliphate tradition of palace planning survives in the way service zones isolate the central court and the main reception spaces addressing it. Inside,

78 **Agra, Red Fort** Jahangiri Mahal court.

the rich elaboration of the indigenous trabeated system in red sandstone often varies themes stated in the palace of Man Singh at Gwalior. Outside, the effect drawn from the same material, inlaid with white marble and coloured stone is typically early Mughal, but relief ornament is resolutely Islamic.

the construction of 'upwards of 500 edifices of red stone in the fine styles of Bengal and Gujarat'. Of these, few survive in the major metropolitan forts. By far the most important is the so-called Jahangiri Mahal, the main element in the harem at Agra,[77–78] and the chihil sutun which provided for public audience at Allahabad.[79] The latter is a talar translated into indigenous terms. Evidently sharing his grandfather's predilections, Akbar had the former modelled on the palace of Man Singh at Gwalior.

If continuous use meant continuous change at the principal imperial seats, the very non-viability as a permanent capital of Akbar's own foundation at Fatehpur Sikri, initially in honour of the emperor's favoured sufi Sheikh Selim Chisti, was the prime condition for the survival of its most important elements.[80–83] The distribution of the palace followed the example set by his Timurid ancestors, but most of the more sumptuous buildings in the complex are distinctly Indian, specifically Gujarati, in structure and style. Hardly had it been completed when Fatehpur Sikri's water supply proved inadequate: the new city was abandoned and Akbar's court thereafter moved regularly between Agra and Lahore.

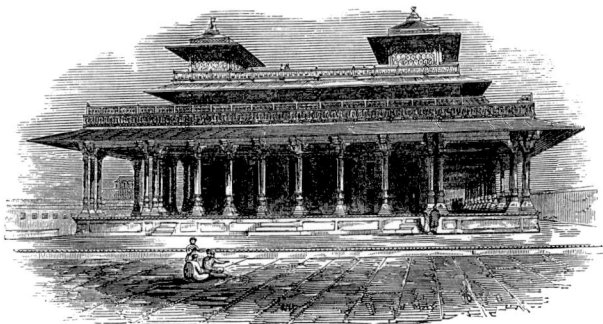

79 **Allahabad fort, chihil sutun** (19th-century engraving).

80 **Fatehpur Sikri, palace** 1570s, plan.

(1) Court of public audience; (2) emperor's quarters with private court around the Anup Tala'o tank to the south and Diwan-i-Khas (place of private audience) to the north; (3) harem building; (4) 'House of Birbal'; (5) 'House of Maryam'; (6) Nagina mosque; (7) Panch Mahal.

Walled for distinction rather than defence, the palace compound was usually entered by the emperor and his retinue through the Hathi gate facing the lake to the north-west. The public gained entrance from the marketplace to the east through a triple gate to the outer court of the emperor's quarters (1), where public audience was held. The emperor entered the audience pavilion from the garden.

81 **Fatehpur Sikri, palace** emperor's quarters looking south.

Occupying the southern zone, formerly enclosed with cloisters between its pavilions and cooled by the square Anup Tala'o tank, the principal court is the nucleus of the emperor's private quarters. Facilities for suspending awnings from its various pavilions make it clear that the whole covered area was often expanded into the most sumptuous of tent palaces (see 75, page 130). The main block of the apartments to the south may have been used for dining and confidential meetings, as well as retiring.

82 **Fatehpur Sikri, palace** emperor's quarters, pavilion.

The northern zone of the emperor's quarters has a range of building to the west including a lavish Gujarati-style pavilion and the celebrated freestanding two-storey structure with balconies, deep chadyas and elegant chattris traditionally identified as the Diwan-i-Khas. The outstanding feature of this building's interior is the central pillar with a fantastic capital of radiating serpentine brackets which bears a circular platform, connected by narrow bridges to the corners of the surrounding gallery.

83 **Fatehpur Sikri, palace** harem.

A screened viaduct once connected the emperor's private
apartments with the principal building within the harem
compound, a large introverted quadrangular structure
where Akbar slept. Its single gate is a domestic expression
of the double-bastion portal with offset entrance and exit
of the type familiar in military works. Apartments were
provided in wings separated by pavilions in the centre of
each side and at the corners, the central pavilions containing
a grand reception room enriched with a wide range of
motifs, mainly Hindu in origin. The carving is assertively
Gujarati and the combination of materials recalls Gwalior.

Flanking the main block to the north-east are elegant

Jahangir was not a notable builder but Shah Jahan transformed the two principal imperial forts and added the final great citadel to Delhi.[84-88] Conceived and executed as a whole, Shah Jahan's fort is far more formal in organisation than any of its predecessors in India's imperial capitals. The emperor reviewed the plans of Baghdad, and though trabeated in structure and dominated by a columned portico, his Delhi palace recalls the great caliphate complexes in an order which extends beyond that of the individual chahar bagh elsewhere.

Shah Jahan's works were usually executed largely in marble, with inlaid precious metal and semi-precious stones, rather than in the familiar coloured sand-

isolated pavilions which probably housed the emperor's mother and principal non-Rajput wives. The rest of the harem enclosure is occupied by a large court to the south-west, probably for attendants, by the Nagina mosque and by gardens. Beyond the gardens to the east is the Panch Mahal: once screened to provide a secure zone of transition from the emperor's private court to the harem gardens, this structure of five diminishing tiers – yet another permutation of the prasada – dominates the entire complex.

84 **Delhi, fort palace** begun late in the 1630s, overview
(19th-century miniature).

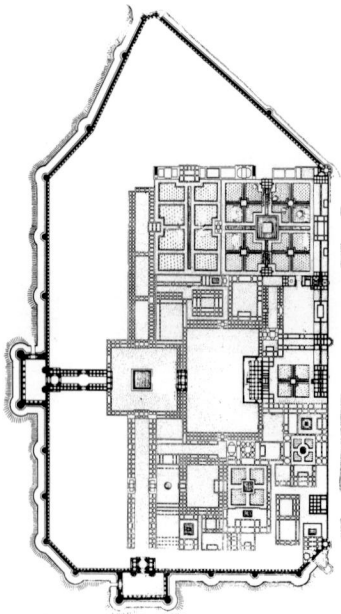

85 **Delhi, fort palace** plan.

A regular rectangle – except for the citadel to the north – the compound is aligned strictly north–south to avoid any discordance with the qibla of its mosques. The Lahore gate, with its octagonal guard chamber, opens the principal axis from the west. The Delhi gate, west of centre in the south, opens a subsidiary axis through a bazaar. The two axes cross in a great square court before the Naubat Khana gatehouse, which leads to the court of public audience with its great throne platform.

The emperor entered his throne platform from the garden court of his private quarters immediately to the east: still on the principal axis, the once fully screened pleasure palace (Rang Mahal) at the head of this garden is the first in a sequence of buildings embracing the Diwan-i-Khas and the private palace (Khas Mahal), aligned north–south on the riverside terrace. It leads south to the now destroyed harem, north to the Hayat Baksh. Running through these exquisitely chased and inlaid marble pavilions with their intricate screens is the Nahar-i-Behist ('canal of paradise') which supplied water – raised from the river in the north-east bastion – to a series of pools and fountains. The cooling effect of the water as it rippled over the white marble was crucial to this environment.

stone. An increasingly feminine elegance tending towards over-refinement was effected with bulbous domes and semi-ogee versions of the cusped arch – essential ingredients in the styles of the Muslim Deccani kingdoms, with which the emperor and his forces were increasingly preoccupied, but not altogether unfamiliar in the north from the earliest phase of Indian Islamic architecture. Columns were given volutes, lotiform or muqarnas capitals, foliate or bell-shaped bases and cannellated, baluster-like shafts derived from the reed-bundle piers of Bengal, whose curved roof forms also found increasing favour at court. In all the main palaces, on the other hand, the bath house shimmered with Persian-inspired mirror

86 **Delhi, fort palace** throne platform in the Diwan-i-Am.
   This great hypostyle hall, its sandstone columns plastered with powdered marble, was commanded from the central bay of its eastern range by a raised platform covered by a curved canopy of white marble backed by Italian pietra-dura. Here in Shah Jahan's time was the fabulous peacock throne of gem-encrusted gold. Before the throne was a dais from which the grand vizier handed petitions up to the emperor in public audience.

87 **Delhi, fort palace** Mothi mosque.

The over-refinement of the late style of Shah Jahan culminated in the garden pavilions of the Hayat Baksh and the white marble palatine mosque, completed under Aurangzeb. Far more opulent than its predecessors at Agra and Lahore, it is essentially non-architectonic in decoration: flamboyant low-relief carving, ephemeral pilasters, Bengali bowed cornice and awning, implausible miniature minarets and inflated, turban-like domes of distinctly Deccani profile all mark the turning towards the effete, anticipating decadence.

88 OVERLEAF **Agra, private palace and Anguri garden.**

At Agra the main suite of private apartments survives in better state than at Delhi. The court of the sumptuous Rha Mahal and its twin, gilded bangaldar kiosks is aligned with the Jahangiri Mahal to expand the facilities of the harem around the Anguri garden – the 'garden of grapes'.

mosaics.[89] Akbar's syncretic style was further developed in this way, though the empire was returning
from tolerance to Sunni orthodoxy, and the last significant efflorescence of the Din-Illahi illuminated
Shah Jahan's pavilions with a highly eclectic range of
royal symbols reaching back to the ancient Vedic ideal
and the quasi-divine Achaemenids.

The garden of paradise
The Mughals were clearly obsessed with flowers.
Inlaid in semi-precious stones or painted in the bor-
ders of miniatures, they infiltrate palace, mosque and
tomb in a delightfully informal way – if with increasing botanical accuracy – yet, ironically, they are
pressed into the service of a rigorous formality in the

89 **Lahore, fort, bath house.**

At Lahore the place of private audience is positioned
like the Delhi pleasure palace on the principal axis behind
the court of public audience – which was unfortunately
transformed in restoration. The sequence of increasingly
intimate enclosures to the west culminates in the dazzling
mirror- and glass-inlaid, many-niched bath house (Shish
Mahal) with its subsidiary bangaldar Naulakhi kiosk.

chahar bagh as inseparable from the garden image of paradise. The Mughals were equally obsessed with water – as were all the rulers of Islamic lands where paradise is an oasis. In the Koran, as we know, paradise is the Eden of Genesis, whose definition is related to the ancient Persian ideal order of an enclosed square divided by four rivers flowing in the cardinal directions from the source of the waters of life in the centre. As a cosmological concept – the context of blessedness emitting benign influence or grace (*baraka*) – the four-square garden is the setting for the tomb and might be enjoyed by the patron before and after he came finally to rest there.

Babur decreed that he should be buried in one of his gardens, in a grave covered only by the earth and sky in accordance with venerable Muslim tradition. The tombs of his successors, among the greatest works of Islam, were modelled on palaces and, of course, palaces – whether or not destined to be tombs – are set in gardens. The Mughals were certainly not the first Indian rulers to plant gardens, but after Babur the chahar bagh is pervasive. Apart from the gardens of their tombs, the greatest of the many gardens of the great Mughals were Shah Jahan's Shalimar[90] and their model on the banks of Kashmir's Lake Dal, to which Jahangir's court retired in summer from 1619.

The imperial tomb

The first great funerary work of the Mughal era, the apotheosis of the octagonal form of mausoleum inherited from the late Delhi sultanate, is that of the Afghan usurper of Humayun's throne, Sher Shah, set in a lake at Sasaram in Bihar. The first great architectural enter-

90 OVERLEAF **Srinagar, Shalimar gardens** 1619, view along main axis.

Ascending terraces, now mostly devoid of their original pavilions, were divided into three zones: public audience, private audience (both full chahar baghs), and the harem. The lowest terrace, immediately within the entrance, was dominated by the Diwan-i-Am through which the water flowed along the central canal, but from which access to the Diwan-i-Khas was open only to the emperor and his entourage. On the upper terrace, the inviolable harem commanded a view of the whole – and, from towers in its enclosure wall, of its unrivalled setting between lake and mountain.

91 **Delhi, tomb of Humayun** 1560s, plan.

The great square compound of the chahar bagh is entered from the west, but there is a monumental south gate as well. The four quarters of the square are defined by causeways leading from these entrances – and from the pavilions which balance them at the cardinal points in the centre of the other sides – to the central square occupied by the base of the mausoleum itself. The unpretentious funerary mosque, incidentally, is outside the compound beyond the main western entrance. Set into each causeway is a water channel interrupted at the junction of subsidiary axes by lily ponds except in the south-east corner, where a secondary mausoleum was constructed. The great platform in the centre contains arcaded and vaulted chambers around the actual burial chamber, which is entered directly along the southern axis.

The superstructure is a rationalist exercise, square in plan but subdivided by vestibules beyond the great iwans on the main axes into five zones, all with their corners cut to effect contiguity – the southern iwan is blind to provide a two-storey entrance hall. The four chattri-crowned corner zones, with two storeys and superimposed arcades in the canted corners, contain the tombs of members of the imperial family. The emperor's great arched central cenotaph

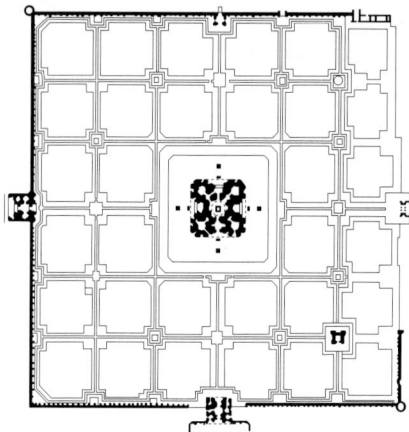

chamber, recalling that of Oljeitu (see volume 6, FOUR CALIPHATES, pages 145–47), rises through the full height of the building. The marble-sheathed, slightly bulbous outer profile of the splended double dome is perhaps more Safavid than Timurid. It is suggested that the patroness imported Persian workers for the job but the beautifully dressed red sandstone inlaid with white marble, not to mention the chattris that punctuate the skyline, are certainly Indian.

92 **Delhi, tomb of Humayun.**

prise in which a chahar bagh played a crucial role was the Delhi tomb of Humayun himself,[91–92] built by his wife the Hamida Banu Begum well into the reign of their son Akbar. Here the mausoleum matches Babur's own description of the hasht behisht pavilion of the Tareb Khana in the palace at Herat, which the Mughals in exile would have seen. It stands on a great platform like the transformed Ashrafi Mahal of Mahmud i-Khalji which, following his conquest of Mandu, Akbar attempted to save (see 55, page 98).

A considerable number of tombs built during the early Mughal period retained varying degrees of Persian influence, not only in the west, around Tatta for instance, but in the heart of the empire for ministers of the Persianised court.[93] On the other hand, the indigenous tradition – especially that of Gujarat – is also pervasive.[94] Akbar's own tomb at Sikandra, on the outskirts of Agra, was reputedly designed by the emperor himself and completed by Jahangir.[95] As the

93 Delhi, Nizam-ud-Din, tomb of Atgah Khan 1560s.
Persian forms were rarely so exquisitely clothed in rich Indian materials (primarily sandstone with marble mosaic inlay) as in this tomb built for Akbar's minister.

94 Fatehpur Sikri, Badshahi mosque, tomb of Sheikh Selim Chisti 1581.

The refined marble-sheathed tomb with its filigree screens and extravagant serpentine brackets springing from chevron-patterned columns below deep chadyas marks the triumph of the style of Ahmedabad at Akbar's court.

setting for a complex that recalls the general disposition of the Mandu Ashrafi Mahal – a site that particularly appealed to both Jahangir and his father – the emperor adopted the chahar bagh formula of his predecessors. The great arcaded platform in the centre corresponds to that of Humayun's mausoleum but the superstructure is resolutely indigenous: instead of a hasht behisht it is a multi-storey structure – a prasada. Several tombs built under Jahangir reflect the influence of Sikandra to varying degrees. The most substantial is the emperor's own tomb at Shahdara near Lahore, shared by the empress Nur Jahan. The most celebrated is the exquisite miniature built for Nur Jahan's Persian father, the I'tmad-ud-Daulah Mirza Ghiyas Beg, on the left bank of the Yamuna at Agra.[96]

Late in Jahangir's reign, the architects of the Delhi tomb built for his vizier Abdur Rahman reverted to the Persian tradition of the hasht behisht crowned by a bulbous dome: unlike Humayun's tomb nearby, however, it is higher than it is wide and the four chattris are clustered more closely about the drum. Sorry relic though it is, its importance lies in the precedent it provided for a revision of Humayun's broad static five-part composition to achieve the dynamic aspiring Taj

95 **Sikandra, tomb of Akbar** 1605–13.

With octagonal minars crowned by chattris at each
corner and an iwan frontispiece in the centre of each side,
the platform is linked by causeways with water channels to
pavilions with responding frontispieces in the enclosure.
The one in the south, providing the only entrance, is an
enormous two-storey structure with exceptional circular
white marble minarets at the corners where chattris might
have been expected. All the pavilions, like the platform and
its frontispieces, are lavishly ornamented with painted
stucco, coloured stone, marble inlay and low-relief carving,
the decorative motifs including goose, lotus, swastika
(symbol of solar movement) and wheel as well as floral
motifs, arabesques and Islamic calligraphy.

Within the platform, vaulted cells surround the mortuary
chamber, as in Humayun's tomb (see 91, page 159), and a
narrow inclined corridor leads to the graves from a richly
stuccoed and painted vestibule in the south. In place of
Humayun's hasht behisht, the prasada has four storeys,
square in plan and the lower three stepped: trabeated
throughout, though with decorative arcading at regular
intervals, the lower two levels break forward in the centre to
support chattris. Concealed within the third level, sealed off
from its terrace except for a narrow window high up in the

south wall, is a grid of chambers with an enigmatic
cenotaph at its centre. The top storey, of white marble in
contrast with the red sandstone elsewhere, has an open
court surrounded by colonnades with screens. On a central
dais, the marble cenotaph is inscribed with verses in praise
of Akbar or reflecting his Din-Illahi, in addition to the 99
names of God. Whether the cenotaph was to be covered
is the subject of some speculation, but given the square
platform and the massive piers of the third-storey grid,
a canopied pavilion would certainly have been feasible.

96 **Agra, tomb of the I'tmad-ud-Daulah** c. 1622–28.

In the centre of the chahar bahg, entered from the west,
the platform is now a low plinth and the arcaded base of
Akbar's tomb at Sikandra has become the main element of
the mausoleum itself, with chattris on circular minarets at
the corners and an iwan sunk into the mass. A screened
pavilion covered by an elegant canopy shelters the
cenotaphs of the I'tmad-ud-Daulah and his wife. In contrast
with its sandstone enclosure, gate and guest-house with
their filigree marble mosaics, the mortuary pavilion was
the first to be built entirely of white marble with gorgeous
pietra-dura floral ornament, Persian in inspiration.

97 Agra, Taj Mahal 1631–c. 1652, plan and section.

Both the main causeways of the chahar bagh have
exceptionally broad, cypress-lined water channels which
meet in a raised lotus pond – the cross-axis terminating
in water pavilions – but only the north–south axis has
fountains. The directional logic in the conception is
reinforced by the triad of red sandstone buildings – the
entrance pavilion, the mosque and the matching guest-
house, which flank the mausoleum. The platform with
the mortuary chamber deep within – a consistent feature
of the great Mughal tombs – is of marble here and the
arcading is blind. The superstructure emulates Humayun's
hasht behisht (see 92, pages 160–61) in scale, if revising the
proportions in accordance with a canon that may be traced
back through India's traditional science of architecture
(*vastushastra*). As in the prototype, vestibules behind
the great iwans are linked by corridors to subsidiary
chattri-crowned chambers superimposed on the diagonals
and to the great central chamber. However, the entrance
arrangement which masked the southern iwan of
Humayun's tomb is dispensed with and enclosed stairs
lead from the subsidiary corridors of the southern front
to the mortuary chamber below.

Outside, the compressed hasht behisht composition is

expressed solely in the arcading, the central frontispiece and the two-storey side bays – no longer with centralising iwans of their own – defined by slender shafts enhancing the verticals without vigorous changes in plane, apart from the canted corners opposite which the minarets stand detached. The dome, more elevated, more bulbous and with a steeper profile more clearly reminiscent of the mature Timurids, rises high over the closely associated chattris and frontispieces because of the enormous disparity between its inner and outer shells, as in the Gir i-Amir (see 13–14,

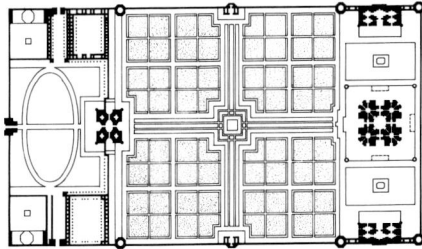

pages 29–31). A dado of unsurpassed richness incorporating
a flowering plant motif – as of the living paradise – runs
around and through the building, ringing the sumptuous
screened cenotaphs of the empress and emperor below the
dome. The exquisite floral and geometric ornament in
low-relief carving and semi-precious stone inlay, which
textures vaults and spandrels, like the black marble
calligraphic bands of the frontispieces, hardly becomes
legible before the relationship between solid and void is no
longer appreciable in its totality.

Mahal which took the Muslim architectural tradition in India to its apotheosis.[97]

Founded in the fifth year of the reign of Shah Jahan to enshrine his favourite wife, Mumtaz Mahal, the main mass of the Taj Mahal is a totally integrated entity on a riverside terrace beyond its chahar bagh where, the culmination of a now clearly dominant axis denying the centralisation of the garden, its reflected verticals are resolved in both directions. In sharp contrast with the red sandstone mosque and guest-house flanking it, this incomparable work is built entirely of marble of legendary beauty, passing through a range of colours from peach to pearl according to the light of sun, moon or stars.[98–99]

98 **Agra, Taj Mahal** detail of revetment.

99 OVERLEAF **Agra, Taj Mahal.**

Moved on from their ancestral pastures by the Mongols, a band of Oghuz Turks entered the service of the Seljuks in Anatolia, themselves hard pressed at the time by the Mongols. Their chief was given – or took – a principality in north-western Anatolia, on the frontiers of the Byzantine empire. Fighters for the faith – as well as plunder – the clan constantly raided Christian lands and expanded its holdings. Osman, leader of the second generation in Anatolia, became a tributary of the Mongols on the destruction of the Seljuks in 1308 but adopted the title of sultan. His followers were thenceforward known as Osmanlis or Ottomans.

Expansion was steady until the Byzantine empire had been reduced to insignificance in Asia Minor by 1340. Called on for help by a pretender to the Byzantine throne, the Ottomans established a bridgehead to Europe and were firmly entrenched on the western shore of the Dardanelles by 1352. Murad I (1362–89) virtually encircled Constantinople with the capture of Adrianople, which he used as a base for the acquisition of Thrace and penetration deep

100 **Suleiman the Magnificent besieging Buda** (16th-century Ottoman miniature).

into the Balkans. His victories were consolidated by the settlement of Anatolian Muslims there and his fighting force augmented by impressing captured youths into the elite corps of janissaries. On Murad's death in victory at Kosovo, his son Beyazid received the submission of Serbia.

Religious zeal and incredible mobility sent Beyazid's army to victory east and west. In 1396 a crusading force of allied European powers under the auspices of the pope was humiliated, Constantinople reduced to a tributary and Greece invaded. Two years earlier Beyazid had been recognised as successor to the old sultanate of Rum by the puppet Abbasid caliph, whose ancestor had found Mamluk protection in Cairo after Baghdad fell to the Mongols in 1258. However, progress in absorbing Anatolia led to a clash with Timur in 1402: the Ottomans were decisively defeated and the sultan taken prisoner.

Beyazid died in captivity while the Timurids were restoring the petty rulers dispossessed by the Ottomans. But by 1420 they had regained all their losses, despite dispute between Beyazid's sons over the succession. There were constant revolts in Europe and Asia, constant threats of invasion from west and east, but militancy and mobility rarely failed. Most of Greece was absorbed by 1446, Hungarian resistance was decisively dealt with at Kosovo in 1448 and Mehmet II (the Conqueror, 1451–81) was able to devote his single-minded attention to the elimination of the Byzantines. Constantinople fell on 29 May 1453 and Hagia Sophia – the capital's principal cathedral and the supreme monument of the Emperor Justinian (see volume 4, IMPERIAL SPACE, pages 208–15) – was converted into a mosque for congregational prayers on the following Friday.

Shi'ism and Persia were the next objective of elimination. Shah Ismail was defeated in 1514 – but not destroyed. Instead, having taken northern Mesopotamia and the southern Caucasus, Selim I turned on the Mamluks. Syria and Egypt had fallen to him by 1517 and he took the title of caliph from the last of the Abbasid puppets in Cairo. But Selim relied on force, not purloined tradition, in his bid to reunite Islam. In this he was thwarted by death in 1520. If he pointed the Ottomans in the direction of their greatest power, he sowed the seeds of decline at his accession by buying the support of the janissaries.

Even more perniciously, Selim's successor Suleiman

(the Magnificent, 1520–66) inaugurated the rule of the harem by acceding to his favourite wife and executing rivals to the succession of her son. Suleiman did take the empire to its height,[100] reaching Vienna and forcing recognition of his claims to Hungary from the Hapsburg emperor, reaching Tabriz and forcing recognition of his claims to Mesopotamia from the Persian emperor, forging a first-rate navy, and extending his rule across north Africa. Manned largely by captured Christians specially trained for the service, like the elite janissary corps, the administration also reached its peak during his reign. And Suleiman was one of history's great builders.

Decline began in the later 16th century as fortune favoured neither side consistently in renewed conflict with Austria on the one hand, Persia on the other. Characteristically the principal imperial wife was the main power behind the throne during much of the reigns of Murad III and his son Mehmet III – and the latter was the last to take personally to the battlefield, on the western front in 1596. Yet the Ottoman tide was not turned until Murat V was forced finally to retreat from the walls of Vienna in 1683. Their long decline ended with the First World War.

The imperial mosque

Following the precedents set by the Seljuks of Rum, the earliest Ottoman mosques consisted either of a single domed prayer hall entered through a portico or a portico and court with iwans and several domed chambers. The domed chamber ultimately emerged predominant and, at its simplest, was endlessly repeated throughout the empire.[101] There was much experimentation, however, and even the imperial formula, derived from the dome of Christian heaven, admitted of extensive variation.

First, the post-Seljuk period recalled the Umayyad mosque of Damascus (see volume 6, FOUR CALIPHATES, page 30), with one or more domed chambers forming a nave in the centre of parallel halls.[102] At the turn of the 14th century the larger mosques had multi-domed versions of the venerable Muslim hypostyle prayer hall, but the influence of the Christian tradition remained potent: occasionally there were nine domes in conformity with the most common Byzantine precedent, occasionally one or more of the domes on the central axis were enlarged in variance with Byzantine practice, as in the Ulu and Yesil mosques at Bursa.

102 **Seljuk, mosque of Isa Bek** 1374.

Instead of an iwan, the qibla is marked by a tripartite portal at the head of the court. This was originally surrounded by arcades incorporating columns pillaged from classical sites. The entrances at the junction between court colonnade and prayer hall were marked by minarets. The contemporary mosque at Manisa had one dome over the nine central bays of a 28-bay hall (seven bays wide, four deep) and a court with doubled arcades to each side.

101 **Scopje, community mosque** 17th century, domed interior.

However, the main line of development was the amplification of the centralised prayer hall under the clear span of one great dome and its integration with the ancillary spaces. A significant stage on the way to the realisation of this on a monumental scale was reached just before the capture of Constantinople – and the principal model for the imperial Ottoman mosque – in the Uc Serefeli mosque at Edirne.[103] By then, too, the court with domed arcades and the pencil-shaped minarets, which were henceforth to be characteristic features of the Ottoman mosque, had made their appearance.

With or without the dome of heaven, the centralised plan contradicted the main motive of mosque design: to assert the qibla. After Mehmet the Conqueror had entered the imperial capital and converted the cathedral of Hagia Sophia, he ordered the construction of a mosque to celebrate his victory. Its design pays homage to Justinian's supreme achievement – the inescapable precedent for covering the vast area needed for prayer on an imperial scale in an often inclement climate – but instead of two semi-domes to buttress the central one, his architect incorporated just one as an expanded bay to house the mihrab.[104]

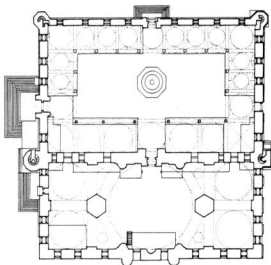

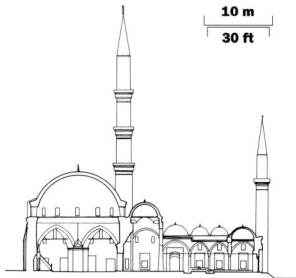

103 **Edirne, Uc Serefeli mosque** 1440s, plan.

The relationship of court and hall recalls the Seljuk and Manisa mosques. On a hexagonal arrangement of piers, however, the dome – 24 metres (79 feet) in diameter – vaulted the most expansive unimpeded space of its time in Turkey. The paired domed side bays, entered directly from the narthex, may have served as lecture rooms. The scale of the arcade bays around the court is varied to assert entrances and corners. With three balconies (*uc serefeli*), the minarets at the junction of the narthex and prayer hall (recalling the arrangement at Seljuk) exceeded the highest of their predecessors.

The inadequacy of the solution had been acknowledged by the beginning of the next century and the second semi-dome restored to the main axis in the
mosque of Beyazid II.[105–106] The challenge of the great
Greek cathedral had been met with capitulation, but
that was the essential premise for advance through
scores of metropolitan and provincial variations on
the theme of the empyrean with which a great Greek
architect, known as Sinan, took the Ottoman mosque
to its apogee.

That apogee is represented in Istanbul (as Constantinople was named after the Ottoman conquest)
by two of the most spectacular mosques ever built:
the Suleymaniye of Sultan Suleiman the Magnificent,

104 **Istanbul, Fateh mosque** 1463, plan.

Mehmet the Conqueror's mosque extends the Uc Serefeli
plan by one range of four bays towards the qibla, inserting
the semi-dome in the central pair. The main dome,
carried on pendentives over the four bays before it, was
at 26 metres (85 feet) in diameter the largest to date in a
Turkish mosque. The mosque was rebuilt on the original
foundations but in a different form after an earthquake in
the second half of the 18th century.

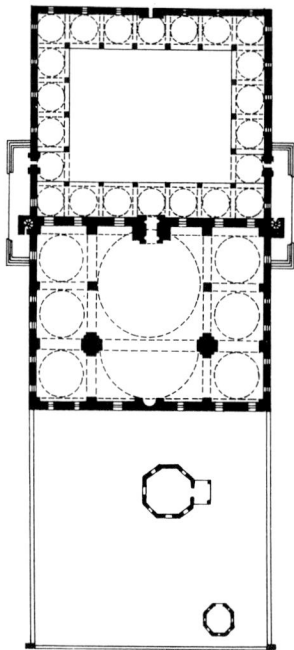

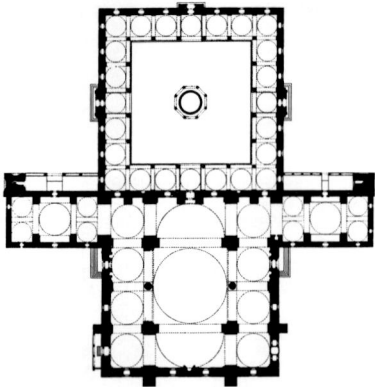

105 **Istanbul, mosque of Beyazid II** 1501, plan.

The Fateh plan is extended towards the court by one
range of bays to make 16 in all. Carried on pendentives,
the dome covers the central four squares. Carried on
muqarnas squinches, the semi-domes cover two bays each.
The four bays to each side are spatially ambivalent: they
are assimilated to one another longitudinally as aisles, yet
without galleries to divide them in height they belong to a
16-part whole, and the middle pairs are screened from the
centre dome only by a column.

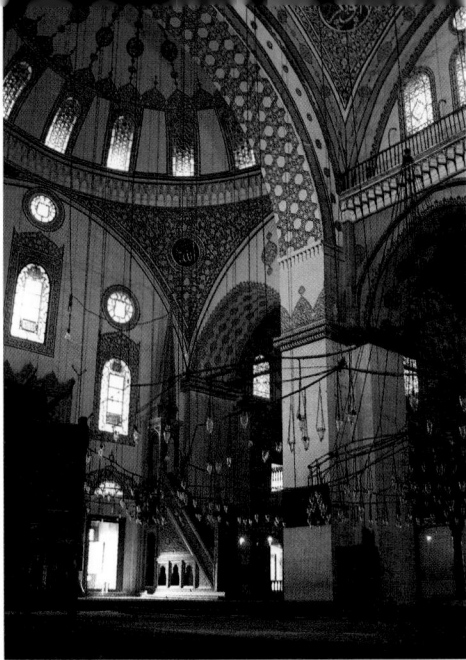

106 **Istanbul, mosque of Beyazid II** interior.

107 **Istanbul, Sehzade mosque** 1543, plan.

In his first major work, Koca Sinan (1490–1588) replaced the ambivalent side bays of Beyazid II's mosque with two more semi-domes – after the precedent of the Greek cross plan already adopted for the provincial mosque of Dimoteka in Greece (1421). After the pattern of Hagia Sophia the main dome was carried on pendentives, but the semi-domes rise over muqarnas and smaller semi-domes in the quadrants, which act as squinches. The formal perfection of the cross, of supreme significance to the Christian, naturally denied the dynamic of Muslim prayer.

Sinan was born in Karaman, probably to Greek parents, and was trained among captive youths for the janissary corps. He served in Sultan Suleiman's army as far afield as the approach to Vienna before being appointed court architect in 1538. He spent the rest of his long life designing over 300 mosques – and much else – for his imperial masters. He considered himself an apprentice at work on the Sehzade.

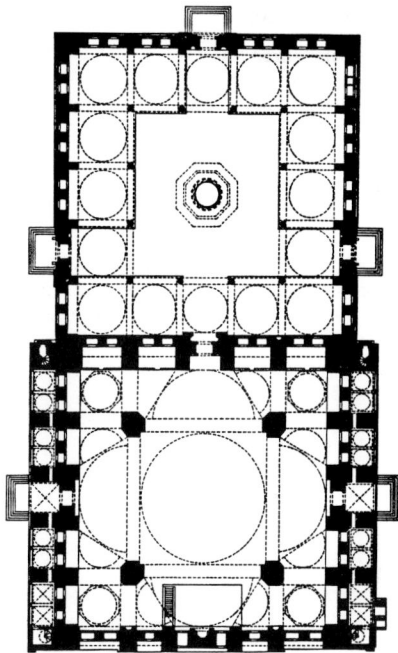

108 **Istanbul, Suleymaniye mosque** 1556.

109 **Istanbul, Suleymaniye mosque** plan.

Restoring a predominant axis, if not the singular
dynamic of the qibla, Sinan clarifies the relationship of
the parts – mass and space – inherited from the prototype,
Hagia Sophia, and its most recent reinterpretation for
Beyazid II (see 105, page 188). The central domed space
is twice as high as it is wide – 53 by 26.5 metres (174 by
87 feet) – and, of course, expands to twice its width on
both the orthogonals and diagonals. Clarity is enhanced by
the exclusion of galleries from the square or semi-circular
ancillary spaces (as in Beyazid's work). Learning from
the structural history of Hagia Sophia, no doubt, Sinan
obviated adventurous buttressing to achieve the
overwhelmingly impressive concordance between volume
and mass, aesthetics and structure, with a strictly limited
repertory of autonomous but supportive semi-circular,
semi-spherical and cubical forms.

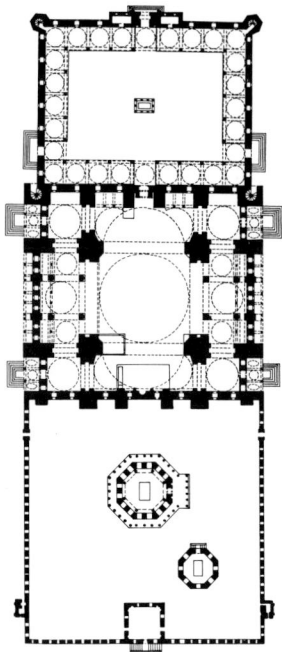

110 **Istanbul, Suleymaniye mosque** court.

111 **Istanbul, Suleymaniye mosque** interior.

crowning a dominant site in the centre of the capital,[108-112] and the early 17th-century Sultan Ahmad I's Ahmediye (the so-called Blue Mosque) addressing Hagia Sophia from the other side of the ancient forum, on the site of the Byzantine imperial palace. Between them in date and form comes Sinan's last great work, the Selimiye at Edirne,[113] which built on his earliest experiment in centralisation, the Sehzade.[107]

Both the Suleymaniye and Ahmediye emulate Hagia Sophia in scale, but with different degrees of centralisation, and harness the organic vitality exuded by its extraordinary mass over centuries of buttressing.

112 **Istanbul, Suleymaniye mosque** precinct with tombs.

To the south, beyond the qibla hemi-cycle, is an imperial necropolis – as there was in the Fateh complex. The Ottomans placed comparatively minor emphasis on tombs, tending to revert to orthodoxy and limit them to canopies open to the sides. They followed Seljuk precedents at first, however, substituting a dome for a cone over polygonal volumes. The ones in the necropolis behind the Suleymaniye are typical.

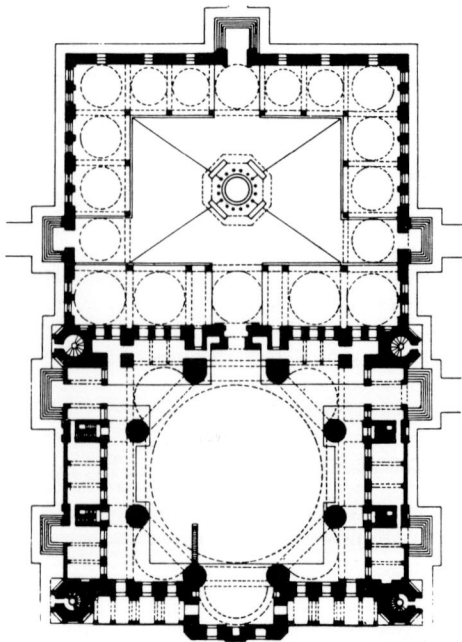

Without sacrificing that vitality but channelling it through an ordered progression of similar forms expanding in scale but diminishing in number, Sinan's Suleymaniye echoed the great domed space and twin apses of his model – and several earlier mosques in the Ottoman capital. After the earlier example set by Sinan, Ahmad I's architect opted for the complete centralisation of the Greek cross formula and, hence, the completely centrifugal aspiration of mass and

113 Edirne, Selimiye mosque 1569, plan and section.

If the Suleymaniye was the masterpiece of its architect's middle ages, Sinan saw his career as culminating in the Selimiye at Edirne. Eight great piers are pulled back to the perimeter of an oblong space on the qibla, almost to the perimeter east and west, to achieve the greatest expanse of uninterrupted space in any Ottoman mosque. The slivers of space between piers and wall east and west are undeveloped, except as corridors, but the shooting of the qibla through the southern pair of piers, opposite the entrance, restores the traditional Muslim dynamic. The four minarets of the Suleymaniye marked the corners of the court. The Selimiye's exceptionally tall minarets – 70 metres (230 feet) high – anchor the four corners of the hall's great canopy.

114 **Istanbul, Ahmediye mosque** (left), 1609–17.

space.[114-117] On the horizontal plane of the qibla neither was appropriate for the traditional unidirectional focus of Muslim prayer, but in annexing the vertical plane of heaven they were increasingly successful in asserting the boundless expansion of Islamic faith – and instead of depicting the host of Christ's heaven in Hagia Sophia's gold mosaic, the dematerialised glory of the Byzantine tradition, the garden of Islam's paradise was articulated in Ahmad Shah's celebrated revetment of blue tiles, the equally ethereal glory of the Ottoman tradition.

115 **Istanbul, Ahmediye mosque** plan.

Sinan's sometime assistant and ultimate successor, Mehmet Aga (who was also a captured Christian) followed the precedent set by the master in the Sehzade but extended the essential rationalism of the plan to equal squares for prayer hall and court. The four great piers are perhaps too great, visually and structurally, and the imperial resources of the dissolute young patron (Ahmad I, 1603–17), stretched to the provision of six minarets – one at each corner of hall and court, perhaps two too many – but ran short of decorating the domes in a manner consistent with the quality of the tiles below.

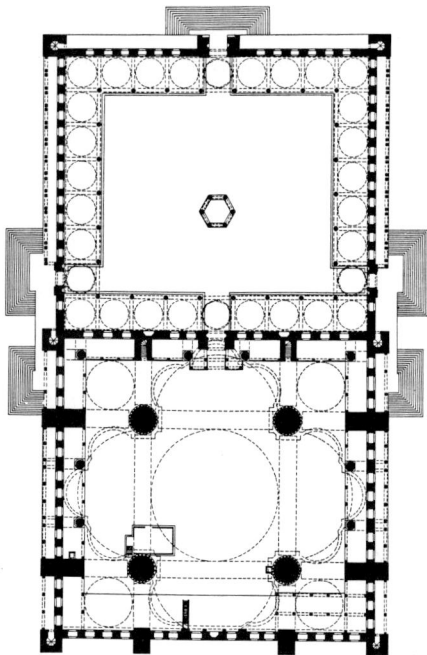

20 m

60 ft

116 **Istanbul, Ahmediye mosque** court.

117 **Istanbul, Ahmediye mosque** interior.

The imperial palace

Abandoning the old imperial complex, Mehmet the Conqueror began work on a new palace, the Top Kapi, on the peninsula between the Golden Horn and the Sea of Marmara early in the 1460s. Following vaguely in the relaxed tradition of courts and terraces sympathetically related to the contours of the site – inherited by the Byzantine emperors from the Roman villa tradition – it grew organically, but the familiar tripartite division into zones of public reception, private audience and harem prevails.[118-120]

Within stout walls defending its exposed but isolated site from sea and land, there were in fact five main courts – a sports ground, two for military parades and the gradation of the public seeking audience, and two graded in privacy – with many pavilions distributed informally like tents in the camp which normally accommodated the patron and his most impressive successors on campaigns. The open spaces overwhelmingly predominate yet, largely devoid of their original gardens (if not their water or their superb views), they fail to impress as they must once have done. Indeed little matches the charm of Granada's Alhambra (see volume 6, FOUR CALIPHATES, pages

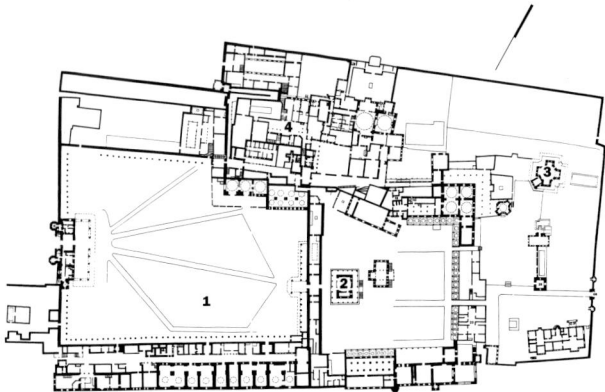

118 Istanbul, Top Kapi palace plan.

(1) Second court; (2) kiosk of private audience in the third court; (3) Baghdad kiosk in the fourth court; (4) harem.

To supplement a provisional town palace, Mehmet the Conqueror began his new palace before the year of conquest was out. At first a collection of summer pavilions by the water, it soon extended up the hilly promontory to include winter quarters which superseded the old town palace.

50 m
150 ft

119 **Istanbul, Top Kapi palace** third court with kiosk
of private audience left of centre.

Clearly derived from the tent, the most important
single structure is the kiosk of private audience (1585)
immediately within the gate to the third court: as the seat
of one of the most powerful rulers the world had ever seen,
its impact depended entirely on furniture and furnishings –
especially the jewel-encrusted gold throne.

120 **Istanbul, Top Kapi palace** Baghdad kiosk.

To the north-east of the third court, the emperor's private
court is disposed for the view from its marble terraces.
These are centred on the withdrawing pavilion named in
commemoration of the capture of Baghdad in 1638, a
variation on the theme of the hasht behisht, lavishly tiled.

210–19) or the splendour of the Mughal court, and the complex's most outstanding asset is the horror of its harem.[121-123]

Depleted in the Grenadine and Mughal palaces, the harem is virtually intact in Top Kapi. Entered past the cells of its guardian eunuchs, it is a warren of tight corridors leading to rooms and enclosed courts of varied scale for women of various ranks: gilded incarceration which left its victims with the opportunity for little but intrigue over the succession to the throne. Most

121 **Istanbul, Top Kapi palace, harem** throne room.

The harem, straddling the boundary between the second and third courts, to their north, once had over 200 rooms about 44 courts. The central core – if core can be detected in this presumably premeditated labyrinth – accommodated the sultan secluded with his women. There was a distinct apartment for the Queen Mother (Valide Sultan), who ruled here – as later she ruled rather more extensively. There were the relatively opulent but painfully restricted chambers of the royal offspring and their mothers. More painful still, of course, were the cubicles of the host of the childless, hardly to be distinguished even by their furnishing from the cells of the eunuchs who guarded the claustrophobic establishment.

122 **Istanbul, Top Kapi palace, harem** prince's chamber.

123 **Istanbul, Top Kapi palace, harem** corridor.

Islamic dynasties ultimately succumbed to the debilitating effects of the harem's fetid atmosphere, but nowhere else in the world can one better see why. The 19th-century rulers left for the delirious Dolmabache – but that is another world and it was too late.[124]

124 **Istanbul, Dolmabache palace** mid 19th century.

glossary

AISLE side passage of a basilica or temple, running parallel to the nave and separated from it by COLUMNS or PIERS.

AMBULATORY semi-circular or polygonal arcade or walkway.

APADANA columned HYPOSTYLE HALL, usually square in plan, with a PORTICO to one or more sides.

APSE semi-circular domed or vaulted space, especially at one end of a basilica.

ARCADE series of arches supported by COLUMNS, sometimes paired and covered so as to form a walkway.

ARCHITRAVE one of the three principal elements of an ENTABLATURE, positioned immediately above the CAPITAL of a COLUMN, and supporting the FRIEZE and CORNICE.

ATRIUM entrance hall or courtyard, usually open to the sky.

BAGH garden.

BALUSTER short COLUMN or pillar, usually bulbous towards the base, supporting a rail.

BALUSTRADE a row of BALUSTERS supporting a rail.

BANGALDAR Bengali curved roof.

BARBICAN fortified structure at the entry to a town or city, often straddling a gateway.

BASTION structure projecting from the angle of a defensive wall, enabling enhanced vision and mobility for a garrison.

BATTERING reinforcement of wall bases by building a sloping supporting structure.

BAY one of a series of compartments of the interior of a building, the divisions being created by PIERS or COLUMNS, for example.

BEAM horizontal element in, for instance, a TRABEATED structure.

BUTTRESS support, usually stone, built against a wall to reinforce or take load.

CANNELLATED channelled or fluted.

CAPITAL top part of a COLUMN, supporting the ENTABLATURE.

CARAVANSERAI enclosure providing overnight accommodation for travellers.

CENOTAPH funerary monument remote from the location of the remains of those commemorated.

CHADYA awning, eave.

CHAHAR BAGH formal garden, ideally square and divided into four smaller squares by axial paths or canals.

CHASED ornamented with embossing or engraving.

CHATTRI umbrella-shaped dome or PAVILION, sometimes acting as a TURRET on the roof of a STUPA.

CHIHIL SUTUN many-columned (literally forty columns) PAVILION or hall.

CITADEL fortress, usually at the highest part of a town.

CLERESTORY windowed upper level providing light for a double-storey interior.

CLOISTER covered ARCADE, often running around the perimeter of an open courtyard.

COLONNADE line of regularly spaced COLUMNS.

COLONNETTE small COLUMN, decorative and/or functional.

COLUMN vertical member, usually circular in cross-section, functionally structural or ornamental or both, usually comprising a base, shaft and CAPITAL.

CORBEL course of masonry or support bracket, usually stone, for a BEAM or other horizontal member. Hence corbelled: forming a stepped roof by deploying progressively overlapping corbels.

CORNICE projecting MOULDING forming the top part of an ENTABLATURE. More generally, a horizontal ornamental moulding projecting at the top of a wall or other structure.

CRYPT underground chamber, often beneath the chancel of a church.

CUFIC SCRIPT originating in Cufa in Iraq, a stylised form often features in Islamic painting and carving.

CUSP projection formed between two arcs, especially in stone tracery, hence CUSPED.

CYMA REVERSA wave-shaped moulding, the upper part concave and the lower convex.

DADO the middle part, between base and CORNICE, of a PEDESTAL, or the lower part of a wall when treated as a continuous pedestal.

DAULAT KHANA sultan's palace.

DIWAN-I-AM court of public audience in an Islamic palace.

DIWAN-I-KHAS court of private audience in an Islamic palace.

ENTABLATURE part of the façade immediately above the COLUMNS, usually composed of a supportive ARCHITRAVE, decorative FRIEZE and projecting CORNICE.

FILIGREE decorative work formed from a mesh or by piercing material to give the impression of a mesh.

FINIAL ornament at the top of a gable or roof, for example.

FORUM central open space of a town, usually a marketplace surrounded by public buildings.

FRESCO painting done on plaster which is not yet dry.

FRIEZE the middle part of an ENTABLATURE, above the ARCHITRAVE and below the CORNICE, or more generally any horizontal strip decorated in RELIEF.

FRONTISPIECE principal entrance and its surround, usually distinguished by decoration and often standing proud of the façade in which it sits.

HAREM women's quarters.

HASHT BEHISHT octagonal palace PAVILION, usually with axial IWANS alternating with chambers at the corners.

HEMICYCLE semi-circular recessed structure on a grand scale.

HYPOSTYLE HALL hall with a roof supported by numerous COLUMNS, more or less evenly spaced across its area.

IMAM Muslim prayer leader.

IMAMZADA tomb of an IMAM, hence shrine.

IMPOST structural member – usually in the form of a MOULDING or block – at the top of a pillar, for instance, on which an arch rests.

INTRADOS curve defined by the lower surface of an arch.

IWAN vaulted hall or recess opening off a court.

JAMB the inner side of a door frame.

KHANAQAH accommodation and study quarters for sufi disciples.

KHAS MAHAL private palace.

KIOSK small open pavilion, often pillared.

MADRASA Islamic school or college generally associated with a MOSQUE.

MAHAL summer house or PAVILION.

MAIDAN open field before a fort or palace, hence civic park or polo ground.

MAUSOLEUM tomb, usually of a dignitary, built on a grand scale.

MERLONS raised elements of a battlement, alternating with embrasures.

MIHRAB niche or marker in a MOSQUE indicating the direction of Mecca.

MINAR freestanding monumental tower, mainly used to call Muslims to the MOSQUE to prayer.

MINARET tower attached to a MOSQUE, from which Muslims are called to prayer.

MOSAIC decoration formed by embedding small coloured tiles or pieces of glass in cement.

MOSQUE Muslim temple/complex.

MOULDING the contour of a projecting or inset element.

MUQARNAS miniature SQUINCH form used in combination functionally in effecting transition from, for instance, polygonal chamber to domed roof; and/or used decoratively to produce a honeycomb effect.

NARTHEX chamber adjunct to the nave of a building, usually a Christian church.

NECROPOLIS cemetery, literally a community of the dead.

NICHE recess in a wall, often containing a statue.

OGEE ARCH composed of two CYMA REVERSA mouldings meeting head to head at the apex.

PADMA lotus, hence also MOULDING with a lotus-shaped profile.

PAVILION lightly constructed building, often tent-like and set in a garden.

PENDENTIVE curved concave triangular member used at the corners of a square or polygonal structure so as to enable reconciliation with a domed roof.

PIER supporting pillar for wall or roof, often of rectangular cross-section.

PILASTER a PIER of rectangular cross-section, more or less integral with and only slightly projecting from the wall which it supports.

PISHTAQ a FRONTISPIECE or monumental PORTAL standing proud of the façade.

PLINTH rectangular base or base support of a COLUMN or wall.

PORTAL doorway, usually on a grand scale.

PORTICO entrance to a building, featuring a COLONNADE.

POST vertical element in, for instance, a TRABEATED structure.

PRASADA multi-storey structure: mansion, palace or temple.

PYLON monumental tower, often associated with a temple gateway.

QIBLA orientation of a MOSQUE such that prayer is directed towards Mecca: also, of a mosque, the wall that faces towards Mecca.

QUBBA domed cubical chamber with open sides, often a MAUSOLEUM or shrine.

RANG MAHAL pleasure palace (literally painted palace).

RAUZA mortuary complex comprising a courtyard with a tomb and MOSQUE.

RELIEF carving, typically of figures, raised from a flat background by cutting away more (high relief) or less (low relief) of the material from which they are carved.

REVETMENT decorative reinforced facing for a wall.

RIB raised band on a VAULT or ceiling.

RIWAK arcade along one or more sides of a courtyard.

SARCOPHAGUS type of outer coffin, usually of highly decorated stone.

SHISH MAHAL room usually decorated with mirror mosaics, especially a bath house in a palace compound.

SOUK market, often contained within a covered ARCADE.

SPANDREL triangular space formed by the outer curve of an arch and the horizontal and vertical elements of the rectangle within which the arch sits.

SQUINCH arch placed across the corner of a square structure so as to form a polygon capable of being roofed by a dome.

STRING COURSE projecting horizontal course of structural elements or MOULDING.

STUCCO type of plaster, especially used where decoration is to be applied.

STUPA Buddhist monument, tumulus, burial or reliquary mound.

SUFI Muslim ascetic holy man.

TALAR columned PORTICO or open HYPOSTYLE HALL backed by a wall.

TRABEATED structurally dependent on rectilinear POST and BEAM supports.

TURRET small tower, often at the angle of a building.

VAULT structure forming an arched roof over a space.

VERANDAH roofed COLONNADE attached to one or more sides of a building.

VESTIBULE courtyard in front of the
   entrance to a house; hallway to
   a building; space adjunct to a larger
   room.

VIADUCT walkway or road elevated on
   arches.

VOLUTE scroll or spiral ornamental
   and/or support member.

VOUSSOIR wedge-shaped stone deployed
   in building an arch. Hence voussoir
   arch, where such stones are used.

The books listed below are those the author found particularly useful as sources of general information on the architecture covered in this volume.

Ettinghausen, Richard and Grabar, Oleg, *The Art and Architecture of Islam 650–1250*, Harmondsworth 1987

Goodwin, Godfrey, *A History of Ottoman Architecture*, London 1971

Hillenbrand, Robert, *Islamic Architecture*, Edinburgh 1994

Hoag, J, *Islamic Architecture*, London 1975

Tadgell, Christopher, *A History of Architecture in India*, London 1990

Sources of illustrations

index

Figures in bold refer to the text; those in ordinary type refer to captions; and those in ordinary type with an asterisk refer to illustrations.

This 25-volume series tells the story of architecture from the earliest settlements in the Euphrates and Jordan valleys to the sophisticated buildings of the late twentieth century. Each volume sets the buildings described and illustrated within their political, social, cultural and technological contexts, exploring architecture not only as the development of form but as an expression of the civilisations within which it evolved. The series focuses on the classical tradition from its origins, through its seminal realisation in ancient Greece and Rome, to the Renaissance, neo-classicism, eclecticism, modernism and post-modernism, supplemented with excursions to India and south-east Asia.

CHRISTOPHER TADGELL teaches architectural history at the Kent Institute of Art and Design and has lectured widely in Britain and the USA.

VOLUMES 1 TO 9

1 ORIGINS Egypt, West Asia and the Aegean
2 HELLENIC CLASSICISM The ordering of form in the ancient Greek world
3 IMPERIAL FORM From Achaemenid Iran to Augustan Rome
4 IMPERIAL SPACE Rome, Constantinople and the early church
5 INDIA AND SOUTH-EAST ASIA The Buddhist and Hindu tradition
6 FOUR CALIPHATES The formation and development of the Islamic tradition
7 FOUR EMPIRES OF ISLAM Imperial achievement
8 CHINA A conservative tradition
9 JAPAN The informal contained

• • • **a history of architecture** christopher tadgell **6**

four caliphates

the formation and development of the islamic tradition

With its origins in the middle east, and its subsequent
expansion across north Africa, southern Europe and east all
the way to China, the Islamic architectural tradition was
essentially heir to the Roman development of space. *Four
Caliphates* describes the source of the tradition in the
ubiquitous courtyard house, the development of the mosque
as both place of worship and centre of the community, its
form moulded by the requirements of prayer set out in the
Koran and given various monumental forms as the
conquests of Islam brought contact with the traditions of
Egypt, Persia, and China. The book also explains the
development of the tradition in tombs, palaces and
fortifications.

Without doubt, the architecture of Islam comprises a
high proportion of the world's most beautiful buildings.
And in the Generalife gardens of the Alhambra, as
elsewhere, Islam produced an image of the lost Eden, a
literal interpretation of the Koranic paradise.